Robert Rea, Ph.D.
Prof. of Church History/Historical Theology
Lincoln Christian Seminary
100 Campus View Dr., Lincoln, IL 62656
217-732-3168, ext. 2273, rea@lccs.edu

IT'S GOD'S CHURCH!

The Life & Legacy of

Daniel Sidney Warner

IT'S GOD'S CHURCH!

The Life & Legacy of
Daniel Sidney Warner

BARRY L. CALLEN

Warner Press, Inc.
Anderson, Indiana

© 1995 by Warner Press, Inc.
ISBN #0-87162-687-X   Stock #D3900
UPC #730817 207803

All rights reserved
Printed in the United States of America
Warner Press, Inc.

David C. Shultz, Editor in Chief
Dan Harman, Book Editor
Cover by Larry Lawson

Dedication

This work is dedicated to the ministers, some actively bi-vocational and others full-time seminary students, who sacrificed to study this material and help inspire its further development. They were my class in the School of Theology of Anderson University, semester two, 1993–94, James Earl Massey, Dean; and the participants in the Springfield (Ohio) Pastors' School, May 1994, Lillie S. McCutcheon, Dean.

Special thanks goes to the Center for Pastoral Studies of Anderson University's School of Theology and to its Director, James Bradley. The Center accredited the work offered in Springfield, facilitates the continuing education of hundreds of ministers nationwide, and assisted in the distribution of this book to participants of the International Dialogue on Doctrine of the Church of God convened in Sydney, Australia in July, 1995.

Across the twentieth century, Anderson University has sought to bring the breadth and depth of Warner's vision to reality in the field of Christian higher education. At this milestone moment, one hundred years after Warner's death, the university remains dedicated to fulfilling that which should not be let to die. In the 1960s John A. Morrison, retired president of the university, had begun writing a biography of Daniel Warner. His death blocked completion of the project, but the work that was accomplished is noted with appreciation and is extended in these pages.

This dedication, of course, would be very incomplete without the inclusion of Warner Press itself, the significant ministry founded by Daniel Warner that still publishes the good news worldwide. It was the first formalized ministry in the Church of God movement and "mothered" many others that came along over the decades. Special gratitude is expressed to Dr. Harold L. Phillips, former Editor in Chief (1951–1977) and historian of Warner Press (1979). He read and provided helpful response to the original manuscript of this work.

To date the full significance of Warner's work and contribution has not been adequately recognized, particularly beyond the borders of the movement that emerged in the late 1880s. Even inside those borders the story has been told mostly in fragments. Now, at last, Dr. Callen has given us a definitive biography that offers remedy for both those deficiencies.

It's God's Church is at once suitable for popular reading, for group study, and through its footnotes, bibliography, and appendices, a scholarly resource as well.

—Harold L. Phillips

Table of Contents

Charts

Songs

Photographs

INTRODUCTION

This book is a biography of Daniel Sidney Warner (1842–1895), primary pioneer of what has evolved into a worldwide fellowship of Christians known as the Church of God movement (Anderson, Indiana). The phrase "Church of God" is used often today for various bodies of the people of God. Whatever the phrase may mean in some settings, biblically speaking, its intended meaning hinges on the little word "of" in the middle. What was envisioned by Warner as "the church God" is a gathering of believers who are of God, whose distinctive life togetherness as the church and full commitment come from and are fixed on God, not on human thinking and organizations. It's God's church! In a significant sense, the burden of Warner's life and ministry was to place new focus on the "of" and "on."

The year 1995 marks a full century since the death of Daniel Warner. This publication, celebrating this century milestone, assumes that one hundred years is long enough to have developed perspective on the setting, vision, and continuing relevance of the life and teachings of Warner. While certainly a man of his time, in crucial ways Warner also is a man for our time, since he was in touch with and committed to the God of all time.

In addition to providing a brief biography of Warner, this book serves as a study resource for the International Dialogue on Doctrine of the Church of God movement convening in Sydney, Australia, in July, 1995. The theme chosen for this major occasion is "Christian Unity: God's Will and Our Role," a theme at the heart of Warner's theological burden and vision. The discussion questions following each chapter will help groups and individual readers to focus on key issues that bring current challenge to faith and life in a divided church and an unholy world.

Warner broke through status-quo barriers in his day. Those

now in the movement that he helped pioneer, coming from many nations of the world, are still seeking to rise above the dividing walls of denomination, culture, geography, gender, and race to make real the quest for holiness and unity among God's people— that the world may know! So are many other Christians who have and are participating in the "ecumenical" movement, a major concern of worldwide Christianity across the twentieth century.

To read a biography of a leader from another generation is not necessarily to abandon the present. On the contrary, not to remember wisdom of the past is to blunder through the present in unnecessary blindness. Daniel Warner, of all people, would deplore anyone making an idol of him or his thinking. Even so, he believed passionately that God's presence and power can and should make all the difference in the life of Christians, individually and together as the church. They made a difference for Warner. Remembering the journey he took may shed important light on the roads still ahead of God's people.

1

Roots of a Reformation

This is the story of a man and a reformation among God's people. The story has its roots in many times and places. Its immediate setting is the nineteenth century. The man is Daniel Sidney Warner, born in Ohio in 1842. The reformation that he did so much to inspire, the Church of God movement (Anderson, Indiana), found its beginning in 1881. As with many good stories, a good place to begin is at the end.

The End Was A Beginning

Noah and Enoch Byrum talked into the wee hours of the morning. It was December 12, 1895, in the little town of Grand Junction, Michigan. Daniel Warner had just died. Decades later this sober conversation of the Byrum brothers was reported this way by Noah:

My brother and I stood there in the darkness, alone and dumbfounded. It was a terrible shock. Only two days before we had been in Warner's home, had talked with him, and the three of us had signed legal papers. Now he was gone. The editor of the Gospel Trumpet, a marvelous preacher, and the leader of a great movement was no more. The stillness was broken by my brother saying: "His work is now ended. He was a great warrior and fought valiantly. He has now laid down the armor. From

3

now on there will be added responsibility falling upon our shoulders. There is work to do now, so we must get busy at once."[1]

The legal papers in question had been designed to safe-guard the publishing work begun by Warner from ever becoming a purely private enterprise. All had agreed that the work of the Gospel Trumpet Company was God's, not Warner's. It was destined to grow, prosper, and one day become what now is Warner Press, a major gospel publishing ministry that in recent times has chosen "Warner" for its name. But in 1895 the work was young and fragile, and suddenly its inspiring founder and visionary leader was dead.

Warner had been founding editor and the main prophetic voice of this publishing ministry. His death at age fifty-three was indeed a stunning blow. He always had insisted that he was not to be an idolized leader. It's God's church! Still, "although Warner specifically disavowed the leader role, insisting always that Christ and Christ alone headed the church and all facets of its outreach, history must label him as founder and guiding light of the early fortunes of both the Church of God reformation movement and the publishing work so closely allied to it" (Phillips 1979, 49).

Stories Shape Us

Before telling Warner's story, we should consider the importance of stories in general to Christian faith and personal identity.

Probably every parent has heard it often from a son or daughter. "Tell me a story before I go to sleep." There is something entertaining, something soothing, bonding, locating about a good story. Locating? Yes, a good story often can help a person understand better who she or he is, where one fits in the larger scheme of things, what life is all about. A person can sleep better once identified, located, and comforted by the insight, joy, and wisdom of a good story.

Jesus once roamed about Palestine telling stories.

4

Thousands slept better at night and lived better during the day because they came to know their lives and their God more fully through the insight and power of his profoundly simple stories. The stories he told were about a sensitive Samaritan, a forgiving father, some seeds that managed to grow, lost coins, a prodigal son, all little snapshots of everyday life that were made to convey divine truths.

We modern people live in such a rapidly changing world. It is so hard these days to maintain a sense of personal identity when nothing lasts long. Our jobs keep changing, along with our addresses, technology, national names and borders, even our marriage partners. The child's question haunts us modern people who supposedly are all grownup. Would some wise adult please tell us a good story before we lose even more of our very identities, our integrity, our roots, our sense of being and intended destiny? We need entertained, distracted; but, more importantly, we need to be instructed, inspired, located. We need to hear the right story in order to become the right people.

Our Western culture has become so individualistic that we are losing the cohesion that makes for real community. What is a "community"? It is "a group of people who have come to share a common past, who understand particular events in the past to be of decisive importance for interpreting the present, who anticipate the future by means of a shared hope, and who express their identity by means of a common narrative" (Stroup 132–33). In other words, a group of us harried humans is really together as one body, a community, only when we have heard, believed, and been shaped by the same stories. To be a family is to be at home. Home involves a cluster of shared memories and traditions. To retell the story of Daniel Warner is to refresh the formative memory that brought into being a people known as the Church of God movement.

One of the most watched television specials of all time in the United States is *Roots*. It is the dramatized story of the family history of Alex Haley, an AfricanAmerican whose roots are traced in dramatic fashion back across the generations of much of American history to the shores of Africa. There is something fascinating and enlightening about such a true tale. Who we now are has much to do with our awareness of where we have been. Alasdair MacIntyre says it well: "I can only answer the question 'What am I to do?' if I can answer the prior question, 'Of what story or stories do I find myself a part?'"[2]

With the right stories, maybe we again can be a community of real understanding and power. Maybe we can find out who we are and who we are supposed to be. Maybe we can be strength to each other. If these stories happen to root in what God has done in Christ and the kind of people that we should and can be in light of Christ, the community that we would become would be the church!

Reform movements in church history focus on attempts to retell the church's story to the church in hope that its members may rediscover their true identity and thus really be the church again. How often we Christians tend to forget from whence we came and who we are supposed to be!

Christian people base their faith on the biblical story of God in Jesus Christ. The belief is that God has allowed true knowledge of the divine to reach us ordinary and sinful human beings through key events in our human history. God has chosen to be with us humans in the midst of the joys and tragedies of our living. Especially in the life, death, and resurrection of Jesus, God has come, been revealed, brought forgiveness and hope, shown the way, given the challenge, opened the future. What a heritage, what a life-changing story this is!

But there is more. God's people have continued to live through the centuries, trying to understand and put into practice the formative story of what God has done in Christ. Never have such people been left alone. The Spirit of God has remained to help the story be told again and again, to help believers understand its current implications, to enable it to become fresh reality in different times and places. Those who have heard and been faithful have themselves expanded the

6

treasury of the Christ-story with the light of their own lives in Christ. Through these lives God still comes, still enlightens, locates, and comforts, still shows the way. When we choose by grace to be "in Christ," allowing his story to shape our stories, life takes on a meaning that motivates. Life becomes mission and ministry. It finds community with other hearers and believers. We come to have spiritual roots. We find that we are one with each other in a common identity. We, therefore, can live and serve together as God's people in the world.

Stories slip from memory unless they keep getting told. We read and reread the Bible, for instance, because we dare not forget. "Tell me the old, old story" says that wonderful Christian song. We also need to read the lives of those who have walked the Christian path ahead of us. Many of them have left behind their own stories of battles fought and lessons learned.[3] Their testimonies are our treasures.

How are we to know what we are to do in a chaotic time like the closing years of the twentieth century? We will not manage to know what to do until we know who we are, whose we are, until we know what stories have shaped and should keep shaping our lives. We cannot afford to forget.

We people of faith should be intentional about what in the past will be allowed to form our future. It has been typical of Americans to debunk the past as something we now have an opportunity to get beyond. Testimonies, however, can be streaks of light from a past that can still brighten the future. Memory can be meaningful, life-forming, community-building.

One Hundred Years Later

The following pages tell the story of Daniel Sidney Warner. His story has been a primary shaping force in the history of a people of God known as the Church of God movement (Anderson, Indiana). This movement, like so many others today, is in danger of losing its history, and thus its special identity and particular mission. The soul of this movement for church renewal rests in part in remembering gratefully the commitments and accomplishments of this man. Warner died in 1895 and this writing comes in 1995. The one-hundredth anniversary of the death of this gifted and dedicated servant of God is a good time to retell his story. Maybe in some ways it can be our story again. In many ways it should be.

One example of the past forming the present is Pacific Bible College. Founded in Spokane, Washington, in 1937 and moved to Portland, Oregon, in 1940, this school soon faced a critical time of self-analysis and change. In 1959 it decided to enlarge its curriculum, broaden its vision, and reach for full regional accreditation. Representing this new era for the school would be the change of the institution's name to Warner Pacific College. Why adopt the name of Daniel Warner? The reason given for the new name at that transitional time was to honor Warner, "pioneer minister of the church ... teacher, poet, author, printer ... who understood holiness in ethical terms" and who was "a fervent advocate of the restoration of the true catholic church founded by Christ."[4] The story of what Warner was remembered as having represented earlier was what this school now wanted as its own story.[5]

From its beginning this movement of the Church of God has been unusually sensitive to the danger of human usurpings of divine prerogatives. It has known itself to be part of a reforming force in an often apostate Christian community. It has relied on the sanctifying power of God and insisted that such power has major implications for how believers are to live and how they are to be together as a united church for the sake of effective mission in the world. Traditionally, inspiration for such vision, reliance, and resolve has been found in the story of Daniel Warner, including his influential books and beloved hymn lyrics.

In a historical if not a theological sense, Warner is a primary "root" of the Church of God movement. Remembering is vital to continued life and growth. Going back in memory, however, must not mean escaping the present by dwelling inordinately in some yesterday. We look to Warner for the fire of his vision, not for the ashes that are only incidentals of his time. To succumb to any stale pool of mere nostalgia for the supposed simplicities and purities of "pioneer" times tends to be a false and fruitless affection. Even so, to lose memory is to lose identity. To be a "movement" is to have roots in the past without being immobilized by that past. It is to be grasped by the intent of a parable without speculating about its incidental details. It is to hear the divine voice without being distracted by the frailty of the human agent.

William Barclay comments of Matthew 11:11 this way: "Let a man never be discouraged in the church if a dream he had dreamed and for which he has toiled is never worked out before the end of the day. God needed John [the Baptist]. God needs his signposts who can point man on the way, although they themselves cannot ever reach the goal."[6] A dream is a visionary story that pulls one forward, upward. Daniel Warner had a dream that only found partial fulfillment in his day. He has become a signpost that still can point us on our way to pursuing that dream in our setting and time. But we must know the dream. We again must hear and be shaped by his story.

A Movement and a Man

A church building in Michigan carries this inscription on its cornerstone: "The Church of God, Founded A. D. 30." The intent is to convey to the public something vital about the congregation that worships there. The message is, "Herein meets a group of people who claim a direct link between their fellowship and that first community of followers of Jesus Christ that originated on the Day of Pentecost. They declare themselves to be a visible local manifestation of the universal Church which Christ founded and kept in the name of his Father" (J. Smith 1980, ix). What, then, is the relationship between A. D. 30 and A. D. 1880, between the founding Christ and the pioneering work of Daniel Warner?

The Church of God movement (Anderson, Indiana), to be its divinely intended self today, must know the story of Daniel Warner. In the character of a true "movement," this body of God's people has sought identity with the whole of God's people. It chooses, therefore, not to think of itself as having fixed boundaries of creed or organization, and it does not consider itself to have had a "founder." The preference is to think of the movement's prominent early visionaries and leaders as "pioneers" in the service of the only church there is, the one founded by Christ in the first century.[7] Even so, while not a founder, Warner's story lies close to the heart of this movement. To forget is to change, possibly to be lost.

Without question the most prominent of the movement's early pioneers was Daniel S. Warner (1842–1895). He emerged as a prophetic voice within the larger holiness movement of the last quarter of the nineteenth century. Sounding much like the more well-known Alexander Campbell (1788–1866), Warner rejected the status quo of a denominationalized Christian community and called for the sheep of God to "come out" into the true church of the Bible that existed long before the divisiveness of denominations and is God's only family. But Warner differed from Campbell. Whereas Campbell "sought to eradicate pluralism and unite God's people by recovering the doctrines, forms, and structures of the primitive church" (Allen/Hughes 143), holiness people like Warner saw in the sanctifying work of God's Spirit the only dynamic that can enable the fullness of Christian life and the wholeness of the Christian community, the church.

The Church of God movement that developed from such pioneering work as Warner's has sought to avoid excessive focus on the importance of gifted individuals and church institutions. This is true even though, in its earliest years, on occasion the critics of the movement called its members "Warnerites." Such a designation defies all that Warner and the movement stands for.

The movement's intent has been to give priority to the presence and governing power of the Holy Spirit. Nonetheless, the name of Warner has remained prominent in the movement's life. His story has been judged a precious legacy not to be forgotten (or uncritically copied). There is, for instance, Warner Press in Anderson, Indiana, Warner Memorial University in Eastland, Texas (closed in 1933), Warner Pacific

College in Portland, Oregon, Warner Southern College in Lake Wales, Florida, Warner Memorial Camp Meeting and Grounds in Grand Junction, Michigan, Warner Auditorium in Anderson, Indiana (where the general services of the movement's international camp meeting are convened each summer), and so forth.

In addition, in the few instances when this movement has been discussed by the larger Christian community, the "founding" name of Warner tends to be featured. For example, The *Dictionary of Christianity in America* takes note of Warner, identifies him as "founder of the Church of God (Anderson, Indiana)," and says: "Warner began to organize like-minded individuals into a new movement that propagated its [new Church of God movement's] message by means of 'the flying scroll' (the magazine) and 'flying messengers' (wide-ranging itinerant evangelists)" (1990, 1,235). It is assumed by such non-movement historians that Warner "organized" this movement, even though Warner thought of himself merely as an instrument of God's work and not the founder of another Christian organization inappropriately calling itself a "church." His understanding was that God intended to inspire a return by true Christians to the one and only church that had its origins in the Pentecost events recorded in the Acts of the Apostles. In the final analysis, one should look to AD 30, not to the 1860s through the 1890s when Warner was alive and pioneering for God.

Neither the holiness movement of the nineteenth century nor the Church of God movement of the twentieth century can be understood adequately without consideration of the life and ministry of Daniel Warner. In turn, his story cannot be understood apart from the volatile setting in which it occurred. Chapter two of this book reviews the nineteenth-century setting, while chapters three through eight retell the dramatic story of Warner's life and ministry. The final chapter explores the lingering legacy of Warner, a Christ-story that still may have great meaning for today's church.

Adam Came First

As with the whole human race, so the story of Daniel Warner begins with Adam. In this case it is Adam Warner. Adam and his family moved from Virginia to Frederick, Maryland, where his son, David, was born on June 6, 1803. Adam fought in the War of 1812, caught the pioneering spirit of the times and moved again, this time westward over the Allegheny Mountains into eastern Ohio. It was a migration drama being played out by thousands of families who forever would remain in the forgotten mists of history. Not so for the family name of Warner.

Adam Warner lived in Stark County, Ohio, until his death in about 1845. In 1823 his son David married Leah Dierdorf (1805–1876). The Dierdorfs also had moved westward, in their case from York, Pennsylvania. Seven years after their marriage, David and Leah moved to Wayne County, Ohio, just west of Stark, then on to Portage County, and finally in 1836 they settled in the town of Bristol (now Marshallville) in Wayne County. Here David went into the tavern business for eight years. It was hardly an ideal setting to raise a family, but that is how it was to be.

Soon there were four Warner sons in Bristol. Adam was named for his grandfather. The others were Lewis, Joseph, and John, who died at age twenty. They were boys who were being reared "among the liquor bottles, always under the feet of the ruffians who were the patrons of the place" (Morrison, June 9, 1974, 12). Then came son number five, Daniel, born June 25, 1842. Later there would be a sixth child, a daughter named Samantha. Five of these six children lived largely unrecorded lives; but, according to Andrew Byers, Daniel Warner was "destined to be one of the principal instruments of God's hands to produce a shaking in the ranks of spiritual Israel, and to lead the hosts of the Lord back to Zion from their wanderings in the wilderness of denominationalism" (1921, 34).

The America of 1842, the year of Daniel's birth, was a

young nation trying to grow up quickly. By 1840 the westward movement had carried large numbers of Americans to the banks of the Mississippi River. Gold was discovered at Sutter's Mill, California, in 1848, and the ensuing gold rush created a migration spectacle not seen before on the North American continent. Faith and hope mixed with ambition, desperation, or plain greed to drive thousands westward toward a glittering but risky unknown. Railroads were reaching west. Nebraska, soon to become a state and the scene of early home missionary work by Daniel Warner, was still largely a mixture of Indians and immigrants. Meanwhile, cities were springing to life across this rich and diverse land, bringing with them both the wealth and misery of the industrial age.

Energy was evident everywhere. Rugged individualism, so common, had its negative impact on the religious scene. Denominational rivalries often were intense, acrimonious, even violent. The Third Great Awakening (1857–59), the terrible Civil War (1861–65), and the beginnings of the "Holiness Movement" all would leave their marks of pain and hope, division and renewal. By midcentury the country was speeding up and the great religious revival that had lasted some fifty years was slowing down. Prophetic voices were being raised in the Christian community, each significant for what was to follow. Among them were John Winebrenner, Alexander Campbell, Phoebe Palmer, and Charles Finney.

In the debt of each of these and many others was Daniel Warner. While the country was being catapulted into the industrial age with its kingdoms of commerce expanding, "D. S. Warner would be absorbed in building another kingdom with an insatiable passion" (Hetrick 4).

The beginnings of the life of Warner were rather ordinary, even obscure, but his voice was destined to be prophetic and his impact one day would be worldwide. Unfolding the drama of this prophetic tradition takes one back to the early decades of the nationhood of the United States, the years soon after its independence had been gained from England. As the young nation searched for stability and identity, the much older community of Christian believers was seeking to refresh its identity by various efforts at returning to its roots, rediscovering its formative, apostolic story, remembering who it is supposed to be. The search was on in the "new world" to rediscover the apostolic narrative, the shaping stories, the biblical base that alone make a religious community truly Christian. Daniel Warner had his theological roots in a "restorationist" impulse keynoted in America as early as 1809.[8]

Questions for Group Discussion

1. How important are stories to our own identities as individuals, families, and congregations? Is it important for Christians to know about the lives of great Christians? Has a careful history of your congregation been written? Are you keeping a daily journal of your own journey of faith as God leads?

2. Is it good to preserve the name of a loved church leader from the past by using it as a name for church buildings, camps, businesses, and colleges? How do we remember without making idols of our memories?

3. Is there even today the danger that a leader (a pastor, television religious personality) can so dominate a Christian ministry that the rightful rule of God is displaced? How can we avoid this?

4. What does it mean for a body of Christians to be a "movement"? How can we remember and respect the past without being imprisoned by it?

Notes

1. As in the *Gospel Trumpet*, December 12, 1942.
2. Alasdair MacIntyre, as quoted by Merle Strege, *Tell Me*

the Tale (Anderson, Ind: Warner Press, 1991), 112. Strege's entire chapter five is helpful in this regard.

3. Examples are Enoch Byrum, *Life Experiences* (autobiography, 1928), Barry Callen, *She Came Preaching* (biography of Lillie McCutcheon, 1992), Benjamin Mays, *Born to Rebel* (autobiography, 1971), Dale Oldham, *Giants Along My Path* (autobiography, 1973), Rosemary Skinner Keller, *Georgia Harkness* (biography, 1992), John Morrison, *As the River Flows* (autobiography, 1962), Lesslie Newbigin, *Unfinished Agenda* (autobiography, 1985), and Elton Trueblood, *While It Is Day* (autobiography, 1974).

4. As quoted in Barry Callen, *Preparing for Service: A History of Higher Education in the Church of God* (Warner Press, 1988), 115–116.

5. In 1967, as a new college was about to be opened in Lake Wales, Florida, its founding Board of Trustees decided to call it "Warner Southern College." The "Southern" indicated the region of the country to be served in particular. "Warner" was thought to represent best the heritage of the Church of God movement to which this new college would be associated (see Callen, 1988, 125-138).

6. William Barclay, *The Gospel of Matthew*, vol. 2, The Daily Study Bible Series, rev. ed. (Philadelphia: Westminster Press, 1975), 7.

7. A typical reference from outside the movement would be that of James North: "By 1881 he [Warner] had brought together the beginnings of a movement that became the Church of God (Anderson)" (1994, 351). Very atypical is a "founder" designation of Warner by someone from within the movement. One example, however, is : "By 1882 the *Gospel Trumpet*, edited by D. S. Warner, founder of the Movement, was being read in Canada" (Crose 14).

8. Leonard Allen and Richard Hughes trace this impulse for a restorationist idealism all the way back to the Renaissance of the fourteenth and fifteenth centuries. See their *Discovering Our Roots: The Ancestry of Churches of Christ,* Abilene Christian University Press, 1988.

Setting of Daniel S. Warner's Ministry

Anabaptism (Radical Reformation)	16th century to present
Martin Luther	1483–1546
Pietism	17th century to present
John Wesley	1703–1791
First Great Awakening (America)	1730s–1740s
American Revolutionary War	1775–1783
Second Great Awakening (America)	1790s–1840
Alexander Campbell	1788–1866
Cane Ridge Revival (Kentucky)	1801
Declaration and Address (Thomas Campbell)	1809
Charles Finney	1792–1875
Founding of Oberlin College (Ohio)	1833
Third Great Awakening (America)	1857–1859
Vatican Council I (Roman Catholic)	1869–1870
John Winebrenner	1797–1860
Pheobe Palmer	1807–1874
Founding, First Eldership of the Churches of God (Winebrennarian)	1830
Daniel Sidney Warner	1842–1895
American Civil War	1861–1865
Founding, National Campmeeting Association for the Promotion of Holiness	1867

2

Freedom and Restoration
(Nineteenth–Century Setting)

There is no question about it. Daniel Warner was a visionary, a Christian idealist, a champion for what he understood to
be the highest of God's intentions for the church. His envi-
sioning of what the Christian experience, life, and church
ought to be is understood best when viewed in the nineteenth
century setting in which he lived.

Time of Turmoil

The period of Warner's ministry, the 1860s–1890s, was a
time of turmoil and decay, expansion and corruption, urbanization and industrialization in America. Hard times had fallen
on the country's "evangelical empire." Conservative Christian
norms and values still reigned widely in rural settings; but the
burgeoning cities were filled with a decline in religious vigor.
The breach between Christian lip service and Christian reality
was widening.

By 1880 the United States population had passed fifty mil-
lion, with New York, Philadelphia, Boston, St. Louis, and
Chicago growing rapidly. Thomas Edison perfected the first
practical incandescent light bulb in 1879, followed in 1883 by
the formal opening of the Brooklyn Bridge spanning the East
River from Manhattan to Brooklyn. Meanwhile, John D.

Rockefeller's Standard Oil Company had come to control the American oil industry, a virtual monopoly. Power plays were common and often brutal. Contrasts were stark and unsettling. President James Garfield was assassinated in 1881 by a deranged Chicago lawyer embittered over not getting a patronage job. Then in 1886 President Cleveland dedicated the Statue of Liberty in New York harbor as a sign of welcome and compassion for the oppressed of the world.

In the midst of all this, Daniel Warner ministered actively. These events set the larger cultural scene and often were mirrored by a similar turmoil within the Christian community. Warner would seek to bring to it all a new light. He tried to build a dramatic bridge crossing the rampant dividedness among Christians, thereby openly challenging the religious arrogance of powerful denominational structures. The results were heart-warming and heart-wrenching at the same time. His was a very visible statement of hope that sometimes was received with mistrust and even violent opposition and sometimes was embraced as the ultimate will of God.

Such a prophetic ministry grew out of a vision that rose beyond the particulars of the immediate turmoil. It was a vision rooted in the Christian faith itself and also nurtured by the times. The nineteenth century was a time that spawned visions of various kinds. One was the dream of a reform of the church that would rescue it from serious waywardness and return it to the pattern, purity, and power of the earliest Christians. The great dreamers included Thomas and Alexander Campbell, John Winebrenner, Charles Finney, Phoebe Palmer, and Daniel Warner.

Freedom in Our Land

In 1809 Thomas Campbell delivered his famous *Declaration and Address* in Washington County, Pennsylvania. Soon this visionary statement would be a centerpiece of a vigorous Christian "restorationist" tradition in America later to be known as the Disciples of Christ, with major branches now called the Christian Churches/Churches of Christ and the Churches of Christ (noninstrumental). In this historic declaration, Campbell questioned: "Why should we deem it a thing incredible that the Church of Christ, in this highly favored country, should resume that original unity, peace, and purity which belong to its constitution and constitute its glory?"

Rather than incredible, time and place then favored such an attempted resumption. The earliest colonists in America, those pilgrim pioneers of a "new world," sensed in the air a fresh potential for real freedom. The period after the American Revolution brought the "democratization of American Christianity" (Hatch, chaps. 1, 3, 4). The power of elite religious establishments slowly crumbled, being replaced by movements like the Methodists, Baptists, and Disciples. Ordinary people were taking matters of faith into their own hands. There arose a rugged individualism, a distinctly American lifestyle that often featured a distrust of institutionalized authority in church or state. People now were more prone to think for themselves.

In Christian circles this independent thinking often came to mean the founding of new denominations that their leaders could control. The atmosphere was competitive. Individuals founded church colleges in part to strengthen denominational loyalty, compete with denominational rivals, and resist the "secularistic" influences spreading rapidly throughout the culture. By 1860 more than five hundred new colleges had been founded in the United States. Most were small "hilltop" schools under church sponsorship. Soon Daniel Warner would attend two of these and then be involved in exploring the founding of yet another, Findlay College in Ohio.

Such churchly attitudes and innovations reflected the ethos of the times. Three major religious ideas drove these denominational developments in the young American nation. They were "the idea of pure and normative beginnings to which return was possible; the idea that the intervening history was largely that of aberrations and corruptions which was better ignored; and the idea of building anew in the American wilderness on the true and ancient foundations" (Mead 111).

Given this vigorous young nation and these powerful moti-
vating ideas, a new movement like the Disciples of Christ has
been judged "the quintessential American denomination"
(Toulouse, 22). This movement tended to embody the ethos of
the times and grew rapidly. Thomas Campbell, for instance,
insisted in his pivotal *Declaration and Address* (1809) that
the one hope for religious renewal in America lay in a return
to "simple evangelical Christianity, free from all mixture of
human opinions and inventions of men." The old institutions
and traditions of Europe finally could be abandoned in favor of
the freeing and purifying air of the broad and beckoning
American frontiers.

The theological perspectives of today's Church of God
movement (Anderson, Indiana) are influenced by the percep-
tions, characteristics, and ideals of this earlier American period. More specifically, this movement was shaped by the immediate time and place of its own formative period, the final
decades of the nineteenth century. Those years had inherited
the restorationist ethos of the Disciples. They also saw the
maturing of a "pentecostal" pattern that had come to pene-
trate large segments of many denominational bodies. This pattern had evolved in large part from themes in the Methodist
tradition, themes reshaped by experiences of the churches and
the young nation after the Civil War.[1]

Speaking about the Church of God movement, historian
John Smith says that "the foundations of this reformation
were fashioned in the crucible of real life," and not "out of a
new philosophy nor even out of a new interpretation of
Christian theology" (1956, 18). Real life was the time of Civil
War aftermaths, a time when the nation was expanding rapidly and traditional understandings of Christian faith and practice
were being reshaped significantly.

One potent force in this reshaping was the Holiness
Movement.[2] This movement, much like the Wesleys, Pietists,
and Anabaptists long before, judged the church to have
strayed far from original Christianity. The goal was to bring
the fallen church back to primitive New Testament standards.
The revival call to the church to experience again the outpour-

ing of the Holy Spirit, as received by the apostles themselves on the day of Pentecost, was the focal point of this effort to restore the church to its pristine power and purposes. It gave the [holiness] movement a compelling sense of mission; the goal was to "Christianize Christianity" (Dieter 246).

The thinking of Daniel Warner, one of the holiness advocates, "was expressed in many conceptual patterns which show the strong influence of classical Anabaptism. Through him they were introduced into the holiness movement" (Dieter 253). But this is getting ahead of the story. First, we should recall that Warner's times were dominated by two competing visions. In some ways Warner soon would share them both, modifying each and combining them in a distinctive way.

Competing Visions

Two conflicting visions clashed in the nineteenth century.[3] The increasing dominance of the first over the second created much of the environment in which Daniel Warner lived, in which movements like the Church of God arose, and out of which much of twentieth-century Christian theology has been developed. The first of these visions is the vision of freedom symbolized well by the French and American revolutions.

This invigorating new vision of freedom encouraged people to insist on seeing themselves as free citizens, not controlled subjects. In this "radical" view, society should be more egalitarian, with religion private and not state established, sponsored, or controlled. People began claiming the right to direct their own futures. Through the progress of science, the presumed process of evolution, and, if necessary, the disruption brought by revolution, a wholly new and better future was thought to lay ahead. That future should be created anew rather than being limited by restrictive beliefs and institutions of the past.

One theological manifestation of this aggressive and optimistic attitude was an increasingly pervasive "pentecostalism." Drawing upon the Wesleyan theme of overcoming evil in this life (personal and social sanctification), prominent voices like

Charles Finney, Henry Cowles, and the Oberlin College faculty in Ohio had a fresh vision for the church. They saw the church able, through its own faithfulness, to make progress in Christianizing the nation and thus bringing to present reality the kingdom of God prior to Christ's eventual return. This was the era of post-millennialism,[4] a "party of hope" outlook, with Alexander Campbell of the Disciples movement one of its leading representatives.[5]

The second vision noted by Moltmann was a reaction to the first. It was "God, King and Fatherland," a conservative resurgence in the midst of all the new freedom. There was an understandable fear that an extensive uprooting of the past was a serious mistake. While the first vision championed hope outside old limits, this second vision championed stability based on the memory of original and enduring limits. The first vision was seen as human arrogance that would lead to moral and social anarchy. This "modern spirit," this invasion of the sacred by the secular outlook of the Enlightenment must be resisted by a new insistence on what is unchangingly right, properly ordered, clearly revealed, and absolutely established by God.

The primary concern, argued this reacting conservative mentality, should not be human rights and freedom to think, believe, associate, and act however we modern people judge best. Truth is truth! Within the Christian community, this meant that truth from God is to be obeyed, not altered and recreated to suit some modern mood. What once was truth still should be accepted gladly as truth. There are limits to frontier freedoms! In Roman Catholic circles, this reactionary vision is seen in Vatican Council I (1869–70). In Protestant circles it would take the form of "fundamentalism" as the twentieth century began.

Toward the end of the nineteenth century it had become clear that the church was not succeeding in bringing in the kingdom of God through progressive social initiatives, even if they were in Christ's name and power. Anti-slavery efforts, for instance, did succeed, but led to new racial ugliness in the period of reconstruction after the Civil War. Rapid industrialization

and urbanization did bring progress, but they also were powerful and often humanly destructive forces. Moral compromise
lay on every hand. Soon the dominance of an optimistic post-
millennialism was replaced by a more pessimistic premillenni-
alism. An ideal time of God's reign on earth apparently would
have to wait until the dramatic return of Christ.

The resulting theological landscape of the last quarter of the
nineteenth century, then, was mixed. It was freeing, yet
restrictive, expansionist and compromising, divisive and
volatile. The church had absorbed the extreme competitive-
ness of a capitalist society. Church divisions were common
and often ugly. There were restorationist schemes of the
"hope" and "memory" types, but a growing pessimism tended
to mute all idealism. On the one hand, the bourgeois spirit of
the modern vision of freedom was taking a strong hold
through the emergence of "liberal" theologies. On the other
hand, soon this kind of "enlightened" approach to theology
was countered by the vigorous reaction of a "fundamental"
theology that insisted on a rigid return to a much more authoritarian principle. It was a clash of visions moving in opposite
directions.

Combining the Visions

Beginning about 1880, one development seeking a distinctly Christian solution to this conflict was the ministry of Daniel
Warner and then the emergence of the Church of God movement. This man and this growing body of Christian believers
emphasized a definite vision of freedom coupled closely to a
vigorous, conservative, "pentecostal" call for all Christians to
return to the apostolic roots of the faith. The dynamic making
this return possible was identified as the Spirit of God who
alone sanctifies, unifies, gifts, empowers, and sends.

Here was a man and a movement incorporating in their
own distinctive way both of the competing visions of the time.
The visionary Christians comprising this movement hoped to
pioneer a better way. They felt directed by God in that particular setting to champion their "catholic" identity as members of

the church universal rather than to limit their loyalty to any divisive denominational body. They were convinced that formalized and official creedal statements tend to blunt the primacy of biblical authority in the church's life and encourage sectarian division. This was the freedom part of the vision.

Likewise, Warner and others also insisted on the return-to-the-foundation emphasis of the second vision. They assumed that ecclesiastical organizations usually lead to an erosion of the leadership of the Holy Spirit. Therefore, they sensed and soon championed a divine commission to be formed themselves by sanctifying power and the ancient apostolic faith. They hoped they could help the whole church recover that ancient foundation as narrated in the New Testament and centered in Jesus. These visionary pioneers were determined to fulfill the evangelistic mission of biblical faith in an open and free fellowship of sanctified and unified believers.

The faithful, so this new movement would proclaim, are to be linked to each other by the divine and not by human traditions and structures. Such linking was understood to be central in the Christian past and especially right for the times. To embrace this vision would bring true freedom in the present and authentic continuity with apostolic Christianity.

Whatever the ambitions of leaders, the compromises of ordinary believers, and the deadening effect of oppressive church institutions, it's God's church!

A caution is in order. Movements seeking dramatic reform often understand the presumed apostasy of the past in overly negative and virtually absolute terms (one of those formative American ideas). Sometimes they believe or at least give the impression that they themselves are a brand-new reality on the scene, original, fresh, and alone authentic.[6] Daniel Warner and the pioneering movement that sprang up around him were tempted to think this way. But all reform has its historic context, shoulders on which it stands, debts it has to pay.

The vigorous call for freedom from the follies of denominationalism and a resumption of the priority of biblical faith in the power of the Spirit had been prominent before the time of

Warner. It sounded in numerous Anabaptist, Pietistic, and then Pentecostal circles from at least the sixteenth century. Increasingly, however, such calls for renewal had become especially prominent in America in the decades immediately preceding the rise of the Church of God movement.

Reforms have precedents, even if unrecognized. The Stone-Campbell movement (the Disciples), for instance, from early in the nineteenth century had perceived most of the same dilemmas and proposed some of the same solutions that later would characterize the ministry of Warner and the message of the Church of God movement. Historian James North reports: "the Restoration Movement centers on two major concepts— the concern for the unity of all believers, and the concern for the authority of Scripture alone as the basis of Christian teaching and identity" (1994, 353). Warner soon would champion both of these concepts and then add the dimension of Christian holiness as crucial to the understanding and realization of each. In all of this, God clearly was at work, often in circles larger than those readily recognized by the reformers.

John Winebrenner[7] and the reforming movement he spawned in the 1820s held its first General Eldership meeting in 1849. This reforming body, later very influential on Daniel Warner, abandoned the traditional Calvinist stance of the German Reformed church. It was intensely biblical, adopted no written creed, affirming instead that the Word of God was its "only rule of faith." It was believed that there is only one true church, the church of God, and that it is the duty of God's people to belong to it and to none else.[8]

There also was the Evangelical United Mennonite church that operated a publishing house in Goshen, Indiana, in the 1870s. Daniel Warner had intimate contact with this body, referring in his personal journal (Sept. 26, 1879) to "these beloved brethren" with whom "our hearts are wonderfully knit together in love." These Mennonites provided Warner with an influential exposure to the emphases of the Anabaptist tradition,[9] and later would publish his first book, *Bible Proofs of the Second Work of Grace* (1880). Included among these Anabaptist emphases were "believers' baptism, voluntary submission to Christian disciplines, the rejection of 'worldliness,' the dual authority of the Bible and the Holy Spirit, the church as a holy community with its members committed to a life-embracing discipleship, and strong emphasis on the eschatological dimension for life on earth and hereafter" (J. Smith 1980, 39).

There evolved after the Civil War a significant "pentecostal" consensus on the broader evangelical scene in America. This cluster of four doctrinal emphases, the "foursquare gospel," comprised much of the theological ethos in which the life of Daniel Warner was lived and thus in which the movement of the Church of God first emerged. These emphases were personal salvation, physical healing, baptism in the Holy Spirit, and the Second Coming of Christ. The elements of this distinctive theological cluster had roots in Anglicanism, Pietism, and Puritanism, especially as these were taught by John Wesley and then reshaped somewhat in revivalistic America. These four doctrines of the pentecostal consensus had Methodist-related theological roots, although each was becoming Americanized, radicalized, and placed in a particular restorationist framework (Dayton 1991). Together they provided a vigorous context for fresh reformation as the nineteenth century approached its last twenty-five years.

Daniel Warner and then the Church of God movement came to share most of these pentecostal emphases and their general restorationist framework. Exceptions were the premillennial form of the second-coming expectation and the stress on public gifts of the Spirit, especially the "speaking in tongues" that emerged dramatically just after the beginning of the twentieth century. In these regards, Warner and the Church of God movement would be closer to the original teachings of John Wesley. Wesley, while certainly a theologian of the Spirit, cautioned against excessive "enthusiasms" (Ferrel 180–187) and was optimistic about what could be accomplished in this world by the working of the Spirit of God through faithful souls.

In the Pentecostal environment of the late nineteenth century, the increasing focus was on the affective and miraculous presence and working of the Spirit. In the Wesleyanism (holiness movement) of that time, the focus was more on the regenerating and sanctifying work of the Spirit and less on the dramatic "signs and wonders" that many Pentecostals insisted should and would follow. For Warner and the Church of God movement, influenced much by revivalistic Wesleyanism, in place of an unusual stress on gifts restoration would be the "catholic" vision of a Spirit-enabled unity restoration. Such a realizing of the unity intended by Jesus for his disciples (John 17) would be understood to be possible only as enabled by the experience of Christian holiness and by a separation from the denominational chaos that had intensified in America toward the end of the nineteenth century.

Saying this, however, is getting ahead of our story. To understand the Church of God movement requires both a knowledge of the nineteenth century scene and an appreciation for the life journey of Daniel Sidney Warner in that scene. To a telling of his story we now turn.

Questions for Group Discussion

1. Is church history worth studying? Especially if one thinks that most of the church's past is a sad tale of departure from the will of God, why bother to review it with care? Is it fair to have such a negative view of the church's past?

2. How much is the church influenced in its beliefs and practices by the visions and trends of the culture in which it exists? Are there ways of minimizing the negative aspects of the influence of "the world"?

3. How was Christianity "Americanized" in the nineteenth century?

4. How are we today still struggling with the conflicting visions of free citizens and controlled subjects? As citizens of a nation or members of the church, do we have rights, freedom from boundaries, the rightful ability to believe whatever we want and shape our own future?

5. What is the true meaning of being "pentecostal"? How does that meaning relate to the teachings of John Wesley and Daniel Warner?

Notes

1. See Donald Dayton, Theological Roots of Pentecostalism, rev. ed. (Peabody, Mass: Hendrickson Publishers, 1987, 1991).

2. Note Barry L. Callen, *Guide of Soul and Mind* (Warner Press, 1992), 7–18, and *She Came Preaching* (Warner Press, 1992), 14–27, for descriptions of these times and how they formed an immediate context for the beginnings of the Church of God movement.

3. The discussion of these visions relies on the observations of Jurgen Moltmann in his *Theology Today* (Philadelphia: Trinity Press International, 1988), 1–6.

4. See Stanley Grenz, The Millennial Maze (InterVarsity Press, 1992), chapter 3.

5. Richard Hughes, "The Apocalyptic Origins of Churches of Christ and the Triumph of Modernism," *Religion and American Culture* 2:2 (summer, 1992), 183–184.

6. In *Illusions of Innocence* (University of Chicago, 1988) by Leonard Allen and Richard Hughes, this common tendency is made clear. In time, of course, the Church of God movement became more aware and accepting of the complex restorationist heritage of which it is a part. Note the move-

ment's church historian Charles E. Brown in his 1951 *When the Trumpet Sounded,* 23–41, and the later historian John W. V. Smith in his 1954 doctoral dissertation, "The Approach of the Church of God (Anderson, Indiana) and Comparable Groups to the Problem of Christian Unity" (University of Southern California Graduate School of Religion).

7. An excellent biography is that by Richard Kern, *John Winebrenner, Nineteenth-Century Reformer* (Harrisburg, Pa: Central Publishing House, 1974).

8. See John Winebrenner, *A Brief Scriptural View of the Church of God,* 1829, republished in 1885 (Harrisburg, Pa: Board of Publications, General Eldership of the Church of God).

9. See Donald Durnbaugh, *The Believers' Church: The History and Character of Radical Protestantism* (Herald Press, 1968, 1985), and J. Denny Weaver, *Becoming Anabaptist: The Origin and Significance of Sixteenth-Century Anabaptism* (Herald Press, 1987).

Daniel S. Warner's Personal Life

Born in Marshallville (Bristol), Ohio	June 25, 1842
Spent his youth near New Washington, Ohio	1843–1863
Christian conversion	February 1865
Military service in the Civil War	March–July 1865
First romance (Frances Stocking)	1865–1866
Student at Oberlin College (Ohio)	1865–1866
Married Tamzen Ann Kerr	September 1867
Death of his firstborn, a son	1868?
Baptized his mother, Leah	October 1870
Birth and death of newborn triplets	May 1872
Death of wife Tamzen	May 1872
Married Sarah Keller	June 1874
Daughter Levilla Modest born	March 1875
Death of Leah Warner, Daniel's mother	July 1876
Claimed experience of Christian holiness	July 1877
Death of David Warner, Daniel's father	June 1878
Death of Levilla Warner, Daniel's daughter	June 1878
Married Frances Miller	August 1893
Died at Grand Junction, Michigan	December 12, 1895

3

Pioneer Foundations
(1842–1866)

Daniel S. Warner was born on June 25, 1842 in Marshallville, Ohio, the fifth of six children.[1] His father, David, was a tavern keeper. In every way it was a harsh beginning for a young life. Fifty-two years later Daniel would write this about his own fragile infancy:

> But life held on its tender thread,
>> Days, unexpected grew
> To weeks: and still he lived.
> Why, Heaven only knew.[2]

The setting changed in 1843 when Daniel was still a vulnerable infant. The Warner family moved westward to a 140-acre farm in Crawford County near New Washington, Ohio (about twelve miles northeast of Bucyrus). Here the Warners would remain for twenty years.

Life in a Pioneer Village

Daniel spent his boyhood and youth in this frontier village setting. Sometimes he was sickly, but often the greater pain was that he felt insecure and unwanted, especially because of the insensitivities of this father. The family members were "simple rural folk and not inclined to religion" (Byers 1921,

40). What worsened the absence of at least a formal religious life, however, was the frightening presence of liquor. David could be a harsh man, an authoritarian father often abusing alcohol, then his family. Rum is later referred to by Daniel Warner as a "red infernal flame" that "filled all my mother's cup with pain, and swallowed all my youth."[3]

Leah was a good, hard-working mother who brought a life-saving patience and stability to the troubled home. She inspired the following dedication of Daniel's first book many years later (1880): "To the sacred memory of my sainted mother, whose tender affections were the only solace in my suffering childhood...."

Daniel's early life appears to have been typical of a pioneer community of the time. Some writers have suggested that Warner's childhood was miserable. More likely, definitely facing some harsh circumstances, he suffered "the occasional moods of an extremely sensitive man" (Brown 1951, 45). Many families then were shaped and controlled by a vigorous Christian faith tradition (Lutheran or Roman Catholic in New Washington, Ohio). In Daniel's case his family did not insist on a strict discipline that was justified by strong religious convictions. There was a freedom that allowed the growing boy to indulge in much fishing, dancing, and singing. He was a lover of nature, poetic by temperment, and he had a good singing voice. Life was vigorous and rather well balanced in spite of the problem at home.

Very early Daniel threw himself into local social life. He exhibited skills in oratory and public entertainment. With a flair that knew how to draw public attention, he was known to mount a box in the street and address a crowd on some issue of the day. On occasion his comic antics would get out of hand. One day at school he did something that brought the frightful-sounding sentence of scourging. When he appeared for his punishment "he was prepared for this contingency by having on two or three coats" (Byers 1921, 41). The blows of life need to be softened in whatever way possible!

Intelligent, sociable, and mischievous, Daniel soon was without parts of two fingers on his left hand. One day he was clearing a clump of grass from a mowing machine when the accident happened. Fortunately, this lifelong disability was minor, is hardly noticeable in later photographs, and did not interfer with what would be a significant public speaking and writing ministry.

What did lie ahead would require passion and patience, characteristics shown early by young Daniel. It is said that Daniel "would wrap a coon robe around himself and lie with a fellow hunter and the dogs at the foot of a coon tree all night in order to be ready to take his prize in the morning" (Brown 1951, 47). Years later the phrase "early morning light" would acquire a very new meaning for Daniel. The prize to be sought one day would be the newly dawning light of God's church in a perceived sea of human darkness. But all that was still in the unforeseen of Warner's future.

After living for two decades in New Washington, and with Daniel now out of his volatile teenage years, the Warner family moved to a farm in Bridgewater Township, Williams County, in northwestern Ohio. It was just four miles north of Montpelier. The year was 1863. Here David and Leah would live the rest of their lives. For Daniel, however, it would be only an unlikely launching pad for a ministry that one day would affect the whole Christian world.

Saying Yes To Jesus Christ

Charles Brown observes that "at the approach of maturity a normal young man begins to feel the throb of three mighty motors moving in his soul: love, religion, and ambition" (1951, 48). For Daniel Warner, the first two motors started at about the same time, though both uncertainly.

Young Warner was skeptical of formal religion, in part because of his nonreligious family background, his chosen friends, and his individualistic pioneer spirit. Religiously sensitive by nature, he struggled with personal identity questions and knew the near despair of being filled with doubt about the meaningfulness of competing faith claims. It did not help at all when he often witnessed what he judged to be the hypocrisy common in the Lutheranism and Roman Catholicism that dominated his hometown religious scene.[4]

Religious skepticism and self-doubt were joined by a pattern of self-centered activities not unusual for an assertive teenager unanchored by religious commitment. Warner's fun-loving and sometimes quite selfish tendencies were countered by his mother's concern and scolding. Leah may not have been a traditionally religious woman, but she loved her son and had strong views of what was right and wrong. As Harold Phillips puts it: "The home in which Warner grew up was without positive religious influence, at least in a formal sense, though it is evident that Warner's mother was distressed by her son's lifestyle as a youth" (July 14, 1974, 7).

One night, for instance, Warner's young sister Samantha was dangerously ill. Even so, her brother Daniel chose to be at a neighborhood dance until very late. His mother waited up until two o'clock in the morning when he finally came home. Daniel got what he deserved from an angry and worried mother. She rebuked him for his poor choice of priorities. His sister might have died while he played the night away! Daniel's heart seemed to soften and a real change in his life was not long in coming. In his own later words:

> Then suddenly a crisis came
>   In this poor trembling breast.
> While treading life's poor narrow lane,
>   A solemn line I passed.
>
> Within my bosom there awoke
>   A monitor of light:
> Anon I heard it loudly speak,
>   "Fear God and do the right."[5]

The country was being convulsed by the wrenching Civil War that began in 1861. A painful struggle also now raged within Daniel himself. He had some Christian friends who gathered on Sunday afternoons to sing Christian hymns. He went, always enjoying any social togetherness—and he loved to sing. But now the words of these songs of witness and joy, joining with the stern stance of his mother, were sinking deep into his soul. The inner war would not go on much longer.

In February, 1865, now twenty-two years old, Daniel came to a point of decision. He would yield himself to active faith in Jesus Christ. It happened in a "protracted" meeting, a series of winter revival services conducted by a Churches of God (Winebrennerian) preacher in the Cogswell schoolhouse not far from the Warner farm. This conversion was a real surprise to Warner's friends. He warned them in advance that he intended to go forward to pray for forgiveness and new life in Christ. But they thought he was planning another prank. Instead of some joke, there came to him the very reality for which he now longed. All of life soon would be different.

After this decisive event, Warner always would be a "sincere seeker for divine truth and a fearless follower of the will of God as he understood it" (J. Smith 1955, 23–24). Years later Daniel wrote reflectively in his private journal: "Passed once more the old schoolhouse where I gave my heart to God. Thank God for that step. Oh, how glad I am it was ever my lot to become a Christian!" He expressed his testimony in poetic verse that still is sung as the testimony of thousands of others (see the lyrics of "This Is Why I Love My Savior").

Historian Charles Brown comments: "What Luther found at the foot of the holy stairs in Rome, what Wesley found in Aldersgate Street, London, that experience D. S. Warner found on a February night in a country schoolhouse in northwest Ohio" (1951, 52). Skepticism and pranks now were in his past; in Warner's future was an amazing ministry for his Lord and Savior. Life still was fragile, but no longer was it fumbling for a foundation. The difference was the new knowledge, "I Know My Name Is There" (see the lyrics of this beloved hymn later composed by Warner).

This Is Why I Love My Savior

"We love because he first loved us."—I John 4:19

Daniel S. Warner

I LOVE MY SAVIOR
Barney E. Warren

1 Shall I tell you why I ceased from fol - ly, Why I
2 Do you ask me why I seek no pleas - ure In the
3 Would you bid me give to all a rea - son For the
4 Tho the world may look on me with won - der At the

1 turned a - way from sin? 'Twas be - cause the love of my Re -
2 things I once did love? 'Tis be - cause I've tast - ed life's pure
3 hope I now pos - sess? It is Christ in me, the hope of
4 change that's tak - en place, I will walk the down-ward road no

1 deem - er Ful - ly won my heart to Him.
2 riv - er, Flow - ing from the throne a - bove.
3 glo - ry, And His per - fect ho - li - ness.
4 long - er; Bless the Lord for sav - ing grace!

This is why   I love my Sav - ior, Why I
   This is why,   why I love my Sav-ior,

love   to fol-low Him: For He died   my soul to
Why I love,   love to fol-low Him: For He died,

ran - som, And He washed me from my   sin.
died my soul to ran-som, And He washed me from, He   washed me from my sin.

Military Service and Romance

Daniel did not escape the impact of the Civil War raging in the nation as he came to adulthood. Late in the war his brother Joseph was called to active duty in the Union Army, but he already had a wife and children. Daniel, still single, agreed to go in his place. So in March 1865, Daniel went to Toledo, Ohio, and became a private in Company C of the 195th Regiment of the Ohio Infantry. He was twenty-two, had blue eyes and brown hair, was five feet eight inches tall, a new disciple of Jesus Christ, and now a soldier of the United States.

The war ended within a month of his joining. He was honorably discharged on July 20, 1865, in Wheeling, West Virginia.[6] The early discharge was for medical reasons. Apparently he had contracted a lung disorder while on a forced march in bad weather in the mountains of Virginia. A chronic cough stayed with him the rest of his life.[7]

There is no record of Warner having been involved in any direct combat, although presumably he was armed and prepared to fight for his country if necessary. How does the glow of new faith in the loving and forgiving Christ relate to the patriotic call to march and even kill in the name of one's country? Such thoughts likely passed through Warner's mind as he spent long nights in uniform far away from home.

A call to Christian ministry lay just ahead for Warner, and with it a period of intense study about the faith and its life implications. That study would include a careful review of the work of John Winebrenner, who had serious reservations about the appropriateness of participation by Christians in war (Kern, chap. 7). Such reservations were not part of Warner's upbringing nor were they to become a significant aspect of Warner's later teaching ministry.[8] His issues were more the finding of peace with God and wholeness in the community of Christ's people and less the sorting out of issues of church and state.

The Civil War was a bloody business, a national tragedy for the United States. It tore the nation apart and split several Christian denominations over the issue of slavery. Daniel Warner, nurtured in part in the ethos of this national struggle, was destined himself to become a herald of freedom. He would be a relentless opponent of slavery to anything human in church life, an advocate for renewed unity in the body of Christ that had become torn and weakened by many disruptive divisions. From this service he refused to be discharged no matter what the costs to him personally. He would live and die a bold pioneer for the reunion of God's church, one "nation" under God.

I Know My Name Is There

"However, do not rejoice that the spirits submit to you, but rejoice that your names are written in heaven."—Luke 10:20

Daniel S. Warner

MY NAME IS THERE
Barney E. Warren

1 My name is in the book of life, O bless the name of Je-sus!
2 With sin-ners lost my name once stood Up-on a pain-ful rec-ord;
3 Yet in-ward trou-ble of-ten cast A shad-ow o'er my ti-tle;
4 While oth-ers climb thru world-ly strife To carve a name of hon-or,

1 I rise a-bove all doubt and strife And read my ti-tle clear.
2 But now it's can-celed by the blood, And writ-ten on His roll.
3 But now with full sal-va-tion blest, Praise God, it's ev-er clear!
4 High up in heav-en's book of life, My name is writ-ten there.

I know, I know, my name is there;
I know, I tru-ly know, I know my name is there;

I know, I know my name is writ-ten there.
I know my name is there,

Daniel Warner, now not physically well, returned home to Ohio from the war. He would be a country school teacher. During and just after the time of his turn to personal faith and brief military experience, Daniel faced a hard test for a sensitive young man who was seeking to be faithful to his new faith in Christ. It was time for romance—and it would be awkward.

The test was a young woman named Frances Stocking. She was beautiful, gifted, educated, really attractive to Warner; but she had been reared in an atheistic family. She brought to Warner both the excitement of young love and times of great personal turmoil. All we know about their courtship now comes from Warner's later journal entry (June 11, 1874):

She was the object of my affections and attentions at the time I gave my heart to God. She was handsome and accomplished, having a very strong mind and good education. Her father was skeptical, and the dire disease was transmitted to Frank and, I think, the whole family. Having talked matrimony together and supposing she and I had the proper affections, I supposed it my duty to marry her, notwithstanding her infidelity and her rapidly failing health. Out of sympathy for her suffering, which she claimed would be removed by marriage, I pledged her my heart and hand. But I asked to defer our marriage until I pursued my studies a few years. Ere many months had passed, I began to doubt the existence of the proper elements of union in our case. I took the matter to the Lord and was soon confirmed in the belief that our marriage was not ordained of God. Our attachments grew weaker and soon correspondence ceased, and she became married to a rough young man by the name of Baker. They moved to the West, ere long parted, and she came back a year ago. When at home I learned that she was a spiritualist and by spells was crazy, in which condition she was hurried to the grave, a poor wreck, morally, mentally, and physically.

D. S. Warner, a student at Oberlin College

Preparing For Christian Service

Daniel Warner was serious about furthering his education, even with the romantic complication pulling the other way. He already was educated beyond what was typical for the times. Still, by the fall of 1865, with the sounds of the military fresh in his memory, a troubled romance heavy on his mind, and just months after his own Christian conversion, he was enrolled in Oberlin College (Ohio)9 to pursue an English preparatory course. Warner left Oberlin after one term, likely for financial reasons, to teach school for the winter in Corunna, Indiana. In the spring and fall of 1866, however, he was back at Oberlin, again not completing the full year. Now the issue clearly was more than the lack of money. He was struggling with a call of God upon his life. During this second fall term at Oberlin he became impressed with the strong conviction that God's intention for him was Christian ministry.

Oberlin was a likely place to nurture such a sense of call. At the time it was one of the strongest centers of ministerial training in the country. The great evangelist Charles Finney, the nation's foremost holiness preacher and writer, was then retiring as Oberlin's president and continuing to teach. Warner undoubtedly heard Finney preach and may even have sat in on a class he taught.[10] Full advantage would not be taken of the Oberlin opportunity, however, for at least two reasons. It would have taken years for Warner to complete a formal academic program at Oberlin and he felt "the need of laboring in the Lord's harvest while it was day" (Byers 1921, 49).

Warner turned to private study as the most efficient way at hand to get prepared quickly for service. He felt a sense of urgency to get into the work of ministry quickly and, having no church affiliation yet, he faced no formal requirements for ministerial preparation. So he withdrew from school, ending his brief but pivotal relationship to Oberlin College.[11] He arranged for a room in his parents' home and spent most of the winter of 1866–67 there in intense private study of the Bible and other books at hand. Later (1877) Warner also would attend Vermillion College, studying English, German, Greek, and New Testament. He also was active there in the literary society. Vermillion, in Hayesville, Ohio, was a Presbyterian school founded in 1845. In addition, an awareness of philosophy and ethics is reflected in Warner's private journal. He was an avid learner, a believer in education. Still, his personal choice of primary preparation for ministry was not found in schools.

In the years ahead Warner would justify the appropriateness of this informal approach to ministerial preparation and include in this justification a vigorous anti-institutionalism. He would write that the only credentials required for ministry are "to be filled with the Holy Spirit and have a reasonable knowledge of the English language." He also would express a deep suspicion about colleges: "Colleges are necessary to fit men for the work of the devil and the business of the world.... They are but devil's playhouses."[12]

One thing should be clear, however. Warner's target was not education as such, something he engaged in and respected. What he opposed was a lack of reliance on the governance and gifting of God and the denominational use of colleges to further divide the church by insistence on their human distinctives. The problem, he argued, is that "all sects have their peculiar mark or doctrine with which they mark their subjects. They have erected preacher factories for the express purpose of marking their ministers with their particular mark" (Warner and Riggle, 1903, 379–80).

Being formally trained in such settings was thought by him to be "trained," not really educated. These "factories" were judged to be assembly lines for boxing a person in a human institution and tying that person to a set pattern of human thinking. Colleges eventually came to be seen by Warner as a key segment in the diseased backbone of the divisive denominational system plaguing God's church.[13] He valued education and sought increasing knowledge throughout his life, but he regarded the spiritual qualification as paramount" (Byers 1921, 59).

But this set of emotionally charged issues lay mostly in Warner's future. For now he knew the flush of new faith, felt the pain of a romance not to be, had been educationally stimulated at Oberlin, was deep into private Bible study, and was anxious to get on with whatever God had for him to do. The primary foundations had been laid.

Warner exhibited one personal characteristic that was crucial and typical of him for the remainder of his life. Position and prestige were judged not appropriate goals. Instead, "utter selflessness and complete surrender to the highest demands of spiritual idealism are completely plain" (Brown 1951, 55). Soon this would be seen in his choice of a church body with which to affiliate. His gifts, education, and commitment would have allowed him to excel in most church settings. But he would choose a small and unpopular sect that he had not known before. Why? Because this narrower way appeared to him the closest to God's intentions for the whole body of Christ.

Questions for Group Discussion

1. Early life expereinces are so important in influencing people. How was Warner's earliest life shaped by his setting? How was yours?

2. Can the love and forgiveness of Christ really overcome major questions of self-identity, even a personal history of neglect and abuse?

3. What about Christian faith and active participation in war? Is killing for one's country compatible with the call to follow Jesus? How should religion and politics be related?

4. Romance can be either helpful or hurtful to people called to Christian service. How can the church assist young people to keep such things in proper balance?

5. Should or should not colleges associated with the church seek to "indoctrinate" their students in the particular beliefs of the sponsoring church? What is the difference between being "trained" and being "educated"?

Notes

1. The town, in Wayne County, then was known as Bristol.
2. See verse six of Daniel Warner's autobiographical poem "Innocence" as in Appendix A.

3. See verse fifteen of Daniel Warner's autobiographical poem "Innocence" as in Appendix A.

4. In 1833 a group of German immigrants settled in the New Washington, Ohio, vicinity. They brought with them the German Lutheran and Roman Catholic churches that worshiped in the German and Latin languages exclusively until the 1870s. Warner himself would be the one to introduce English to the town's religious scene when later he would be the founding pastor of a new congregation in New Washington. See Kenneth Cummins, *Dutchtown: A Complete History of New Washington and Cranberry Township* (New Washington Centennial Committee, 1974), 139.

5. See verses seventeen and eighteen of Daniel Warner's autobiographical poem "Innocence" as in Appendix A.

6. It is ironic that, soon after Warner's death in 1895, the publishing work that he then had founded, the Gospel Trumpet Company, would make its home until 1906 in Moundsville, WVa, just outside Wheeling. A further irony is that, although the great Alexander Campbell (estate and college) was located in Bethany, West Virginia, just a few miles from Moundsville, Warner likely had no awareness of this during his military service.

7. At his death in 1895 Warner's widow, Frances, applied for a pension, arguing that her husband's death was related to his military service. But a doctor's examination of the body two days following death concluded that the cause of death was pneumonia, a condition not clearly related to his military service. The application was denied.

8. See Callen 1992, *Thinking...*, 52–53, 59–60, 64–65, and Strege, April 1991.

9. Oberlin College is located about forty miles southwest of Cleveland, Ohio. This campus had a reputation for "liberalism," anti-slavery sentiment, and holiness revivalism.

10. Harold Phillips wrote an editorial in *Vital Christianity* (Oct. 6, 1974) exploring the ministry of Charles Finney and reflecting on the possible effect he may have had on young Daniel Warner.

11. The Church of God movement much later would have another "Oberlin connection," this time at the seminary level. In the 1940s Oberlin, still a significant center for ministerial preparation, was educating several young men and women called to ministry in the tradition that Warner first nurtured. This circumstance had an effect on the movement's launching of its own seminary by Anderson College (University) in Anderson, Indiana (see Callen 1992, Guide..., 157–158).

12. *Gospel Trumpet*, October 15, 1884, 2.

13. Note "Our Pioneers Were Ultra-Supernaturalists" in Barry Callen, *Faith, Learning, and Life: Views from the President's Office of Anderson University* (Anderson University and Warner Press, 1991), 5–6. Warner should not be read as being opposed to education. He was a disciplined learner throughout his life and left behind an impressive private library and a dream for a school in Grand Junction, Michigan. His personal library has been catalogued by John Alan Howard, unpublished class project, Anderson University School of Theology, December 1970 (available in the university's archives). Beyond the expected volumes on the Bible, theology, and church history, there also were numerous others on music, poetry, and health.

4

Seeking the Vision
(1867–1876)

Daniel Warner was a man in love. He loved his Lord supremely and soon he would be active in God's service as a full-time minister. There also was love for a woman. A young man of intense passion, Warner needed a vision to focus all of his fresh commitment—and he needed a companion in full sympathy with that vision. He would find and then lose such a companion; but his vision would remain and expand.

Stalked By Sorrow

While Warner's conversion to Christ had been accompanied by his troubled and short-lived romance with Frances Stocking, his time of beginning active Christian ministry now was enriched by a fulfilling love for Tamzen Ann Kerr. They had met in his schoolteaching days when he located near her home in the vicinity of West Unity in Williams County, Ohio. They were married on September 5, 1867. The experience was quite the opposite of the earlier Stocking episode. Tamzen was devoted to Daniel, shared his faith and values, and appears to have been sympathetic and helpful to his early ministry.

Almost from the beginning, however, their married life seemed to be stalked by deep sorrow. Their first child, a boy, was born in December 1868 and is not mentioned again

D. S. Warner and wife, Tamzen Kerr

(apparently died as an infant). Then in 1872 triplets were born to the Warners, but none survived. Tamzen herself never recovered from complications of this multiple birth and died on May 26 "after a succession of spasms" (Byers 1921, 59). Now sad and lonely, Warner would throw himself into his divine calling, a focused, grieving, and determined man.

Thirteen months after these deaths he would be a frontier missionary in Nebraska. But first he grieved his great personal loss. His private journal carries this entry about a year after the death of his beloved Tamzen and the triplets:

I am writing these lines in the beautiful cemetery near New Haven, Ohio (Huron County). Before me is the little mound which shows the resting-place of my three little infants who a little over a year ago passed in a few hours through this vale of tears, and their little spirits are forever at rest with Jesus; and in one little box their bodies await the Saviour's coming. What a glorious morning when all these graves shall burst open and the bodies shall come forth!... Lord, make me a good man and keep me pure in heart. Farewell, sacred spot. Farewell, little tomb, with thy three-fold treasure.

He had purchased a tombstone in Bryan, Ohio, for Tamzen's grave. Here is what he composed for its facing:

> How sweet and pure in social life,
> As daughter, sister, friend and wife!
> Now done with cares below the sun,
> She shines before the snow-white throne.

Sorrow could be an avenue to joy. Death can lead to life. Warner, having grieved, now would go on, somehow moving beyond human grief to the joy of his divine calling in Christ.

Launching into Active Ministry

Formal Christian ministry activities began for Daniel Warner with the delivery of his first sermon on Easter Sunday evening, 1867. He was the guest speaker in a protracted revival meeting sponsored by the Methodist Episcopal Church in the Cogswell schoolhouse. This was near his home and the very site of his own conversion two years earlier. Here was the perfect place to start proclaiming the divine grace that had brought such a difference in his own life.

If preaching was to be Warner's life calling, presumably some church affiliation was necessary.[1] So, across the summer of 1867, while preparing for his marriage in September, Warner sought wisdom on the question of the best available church connection. He examined with care the practices and beliefs of the churches in his community and sought to compare them with his own growing understanding of biblical teaching. The final choice was a small body known as the General Eldership of the Churches of God in North America. This denomination had been organized in 1825–30 in Harrisburg, Pennsylvania, by John Winebrenner, a former German Reformed minister whose revivalism finally had separated him from his parent body.[2]

Warner was licensed to preach by the West Ohio Eldership at its eleventh annual meeting convened at Findlay, Ohio, in October 1867. His first pastoral assignment was the congregation in Mount Blanchard just south of Findlay. In his journal nine years later (Oct. 1, 1876), Warner was overcome with emotion as he recalled this eldership meeting in Findlay. "I had not expected a license; but how I trembled with fear and dread when I learned that a license and a field of labor were given me!... Having begun an invalid, supposed by many to be a consumptive, my strength has gradually increased through God's blessings and mercies."

The stances of the Churches of God (Winebrennarian) attracted Warner because they appeared so biblical to him. In fact, Warner's "self-imposed course of private biblical and theological studies ... and his very mental furniture bear the Winebrennerian stamp" (Long 6).

What was this theological stamp? It focused on a five-point theological transformation experienced by John Winebrenner across the 1820s, a transformation inspired by revivalism and his interaction with leaders of groups like the United Brethren in Christ. The points reflect roots in German Pietism and other "radical" elements of the Protestant Reformation that had been transplanted to America and had become part of America's revivalistic scene.

By 1830 these points had led Winebrenner to a rupture in his relationship with the German Reformed Church. Now in the 1860s the same points were shaping the early vision of Warner. They were as follows:

1. The Bible is the Word of God, the only authoritative rule of faith and practice. This "only" left no place for church tradition, including human inventions like creeds, catechisms, rituals, and the like;

2. Spiritual regeneration, being born again, always is necessary for a person to become a real Christian and church member. Thus the Christian faith is rooted in the Bible and in such spiritual experience;

3. Humankind possesses free moral agency and the ability, with the Spirit's assistance, to repent, believe, and be saved. Thus denied were the Reformed doctrines of predestination, providence, and perseverance;

4. Baptism and the Lord's Supper became seen as symbolic "ordinances" rather than grace-conveying "sacraments." Baptism necessarily is to be preceded by belief and regeneration and is best administered by immersion (eliminating the appropriateness of infant baptism);

5. Regarding the church, the only requirement for membership in a local congregation is having been born again and the true biblical name for a local congregation or for the body of Christ as a whole is "Church of God" (Gossard 89–90).

John Winebrenner had no intention of founding a new denomination, bodies he stigmatized as "sects." He saw no church organization as legitimate if it limited the freedom of local congregations, which are to accept no human creed, name, or ordinance. It's God's church, he insisted, not a contrived human arrangement in God's name. In this way Winebrenner saw a basis for the unity of all Christians and churches. This general anti-denominational view, when joined with the Wesleyan teaching of holiness, was to become the view, indeed, the vision of Daniel Warner in his later years. He also would not intend to found a new denomination and would insist that it's God's church!

The decade 1867–1877 saw Daniel Warner functioning as an active minister with the General Eldership of the Churches of God, ministering under the guidance of its founding convictions. He would hold pastorates in Ohio, invest two vigorous years in pioneer mission work in Nebraska, and preach revival meetings in country stores, schoolhouses, and churches of various denominations. In these very busy years Warner was selfless and surrendered to the demands of spiritual idealism. According to John Smith, "he was hard working, diligent, conscientious, and more than moderately successful in his ministry" (1965, 12).

Warner had a keen mind, a strong voice, a full beard, and amazing physical stamina for a man always prone to physical problems. When Warner was just thirty-one years old and in ministry only six years, he reported in his private journal (April 27, 1873) that already he had preached some 1,241 sermons, with 508 resulting conversions. Though always contending with "weak lungs," by God's grace he had never missed one appointment because of health. But he did miss his family, having suffered grief over the deaths of his wife Tamzen and their four children.

His early ministry with the West Ohio Eldership included much denominational responsibility. He was elected in 1869 to the Stationing Committee and the Committee on Rule, Order, and Religion. He was elected the First Clerk by the West Ohio Eldership in October 1870, and was appointed to a special committee to raise funds for widows and orphans. In 1871 he was elected to preach the opening sermon at the next Eldership meeting.

He attended and was elected chair of the West Ohio Sunday School Convention in the summer of 1872. Along the way his numerous revival meetings resulted in the organization of nine new congregations of the Churches of God. Warner clearly was a vigorous, committed, and effective young pastor-evangelist.

One of these new congregations formed during Warner's early ministry was in his own hometown of New Washington, Ohio.[3] In fact, the first religious group ever to hold local services in the English language in New Washington was the Church of God (Winebrennerian) congregation organized in March 1871 under the direction of Rev. Daniel Warner. He served as its pastor for its first two years prior to his departure for Nebraska on a home mission assignment in the summer of 1873 (Cummins 139).

This congregation's beginning is recorded vividly by Warner himself. He refers to the town as a place "abandoned to the mercies of Catholics, old Lutherans, and saloons, all of which were equally destructive of all moral good." He was assigned to a circuit surrounding New Washington. So, "knowing the debauchery and ignorance of the people in general," he decided to resettle in the town where he had grown up. After renting a vacant building that had been a drug store and saloon, he soon played a key role in the conversion of the building's owner. A revival conducted by Warner was "attended with great power" and "produced a great stir among the people." Soon forty-six converts were baptized and formed into a new Churches of God congregation. Warner served as their minister for two years. Several of the members were his previous schoolmates, acquaintances, and neighbors.

During the years 1872–80 Warner kept a personal and quite detailed journal.[4] Mostly preserved to this date, it reveals an active preacher and man of prayer, one with a heavy burden for lost souls. There were days spent in fasting and Bible study, others preaching and visiting the sick. Occasionally we learn that "this morning I [Warner] spent an hour rambling far out in the dense, rolling forest to breath the pure air and to hold communion with my God." Right after this retreat, "at ten William Riser's house was filled with brethren and sisters. We had a glorious meeting. All were happy, many shouted" (Mar. 13, 1873).

Some days were not so happy. Warner is candid about times that he expended great effort and did not witness many conversions or the planting of new congregations. For instance, in the year following his organization of the New Washington congregation, he reports a trip to Todedo where he "walked nearly all day in search of a place to open a mission," with the result noted only as "no success."

Holiness, Hypocrisy, and Justice

At first Warner opposed holiness teaching. Here is part of his journal entry of November 11, 1872, about some so-called holiness people at a meeting: "Nearly all blew loudly the horn of sanctification but manifested little of its fruits, such as travail of soul for the sinner and sympathy for the one soul at the altar, to whom none gave a word of encouragement, but each in turn arose and boasted of his holiness. Oh the delusions of Satan!" This kind of hypocrisy caused much searching for a man like Warner not inclined to be patient with the inauthentic, yet a man dedicated to belief in the power of God to change human life. How does one balance the heights of profession and the shallowness of practice?

In place of hypocrisy in the church, Warner was convinced that God intended to bring reformation to a church that had drifted far away from God's will. The very first entry in his journal, written on November 8, 1872, in Bucyrus, Ohio, keynotes a deep concern that Warner would evidence for the rest of his life. "The M. E. Church had a festival," he wrote. "I and a few members of the same church (who repudiated these follies and inconsistencies) met for prayer and the Lord was with us: These brethren were much dissatisfied with their church relationship." Confronting church establishments that breed such dissatisfaction would consume the balance of Warner's life.

Such confronting would be full of pain and joy. Some people would resist and even persecute. The establishment rarely chooses to move voluntarily. Many others would respond more positively, seeing Warner's powerful convictions as the direction of God's will for the church. On March 11, 1873, for instance, Warner recalls in his journal that he preached that morning "on sisters' right to speak and pray in meeting.... House crowded and many on the outside. One brother who was always opposed to women's speaking arose and confessed his error. We then proceeded to the water, where I baptized twenty-two converts in eleven minutes. All came out shouting and praising God.... Great God, what a pity that the

1 January 1879

Since last writing my time has been closely devoted to writing for the Herald and on my little book. This seems to have been the order of the Lord and he has most wonderfully blessed me in the work. The Spirit is continually taking the things of Christ and showing them to me. Glory to God for the new beauties and blessed unfoldings of divine truth, under the clear light of the "anointing that abideth and teacheth of all things". The luminous hidings of revelation seen through the all searching telescope of the Holy Ghost raises many texts that were but dim and of doubtful application to the definite purifying grace, to their true magnitude of absolute authority; while one beautiful blazing constellation of bible truth after another is brought to view untill the adoring soul sees no end to the divine evidences of the "second grace" save the end of revelation itself, and even there the Spirit takes up the eternal theme and writes it all over the soul; on the tablet of the heart and upon every fiber of our conscious being; yea writes it upon the "merchandise" of the Saints all over the entire universe of Gods creation; on every surrounding object even upon the bells of the horses shall there be Holiness unto the Lord.

We can begin to see the effects under God of "praising the beauty of holiness" in this place; in our prayer and class meetings many express a hunger for full salvation; and as we frequently

A page from the personal journal of D. S. Warner

world is cursed by an unholy sectarian ministry who teach for doctrine the commandments of men!" In giving voice to women, Warner was only exercising in one more way his responsibility to be a herald of God's sovereignty in the church of God. Other events sensitized him further to the injustice being done to women, an injustice about which he could not be still. On February 12, 1875, for instance, he visited a village of Omaha Indians camped about two miles from Seward, Nebraska. He recalls:

> They were on their return from their winter's hunt. Were well-laden with robes and furs. It was an interesting visit. The squaws were busily engaged in dressing and tanning buffalo robes; the men stood and looked on. Poor creatures! They seemed to be but servants for the men.[5]

It was not all that different among the non-Indian population of Nebraska at the time. Nebraska had become a state in 1867, the thirty-seventh. Its constitution denied the vote to women and allowed black men to vote only because of the insistence of the federal government. Such injustice was hard for Warner to tolerate quietly. Now he was about to face the Nebraska territory directly.

The Cold Winds of Nebraska

On June 25, 1873, Daniel Warner set out by train for his new mission assignment in Seward, Nebraska. He already was an effective evangelist and a proven church planter. Now his denomination called for his services in this difficult frontier place, probably in part because he was enthusiastic, young, and without family. Warner's journal (May 23) carries his personal reflections on this big change in his life and ministry. "Again I lay all upon the altar of God. It is very hard for me to leave my dearly beloved brethren of West Ohio. Thank God the great Head of the church is with them and his cause is greatly prospering here, and I must go to help the cause in the far west; we parted with tears and many tender farewells."

One other source of tears was very real. He faced the first anniversary of the death of his wife Tamzen and triplet babies. "How lonely I feel!" are the words he confessed to his journal on May 28. "My bereavement comes with all its weight upon me. Lord, be thou my comforter in all my loneliness." Before leaving for the West, he arranged to correspond with a Sarah Keller of Upper Sandusky, Ohio, someone he refers to as "a kind friend." Apparently Sarah was soon seen as the way the Lord would choose to comfort Warner in his loneliness. She was only eighteen but was mature, sensitive, and offered timely sympathy to Daniel. Her father, a successful farmer, was a devout Christian associated with the Churches of God. From this correspondence "soon sprang a glowing flame of love, the beginning of a companionship that meant for him so much of both weal and woe" (Byers 1921, 77).

The departure of Warner for Nebraska was accompanied by a prayer committed only to the privacy of his journal: "Thirty-one years of my hasty life have passed away. O Lord, whatever has not been set down to thy glory, for Jesus' sake, blot out through the blood of Christ. Only eight years have been devoted to God and they crowded with many imperfections. Wash me Lord and make me clean. Keep me pure in heart that the remainder of my life may be all given to God."

Now Warner was on the road west for God. Many new experiences would quickly come his way. He paid $9.40 for his one-way rail ticket to Nebraska and soon was being awed by the big buildings of Chicago. On July 3 he crossed the Missouri River to Nebraska City on the steamer Lizzie Campbell. It was just in time to get in on the local independence day celebrations. Thirty-seven young women, accompanied by a band, were dressed in white, each wearing a badge of one of the thirty-seven states (Nebraska was the newest).

Warner landed on the Nebraska plains "with his Bible, his pony and buggy, and his heart all aflame with love—first to God, and second to pretty Sarah Keller" (Morrison, Aug. 11, 1974, 10). He preached his first sermon two days later and then launched into a hectic ministry schedule. His work was in five counties in the region that lay south of the Platte River between the two cities of Grand Island and Lincoln. Here is where most of the people lived in this new state. Roads were nearly nonexistent. Many of the people were recent settlers living in sod huts and dugouts, barely fit for human habitation. Warner's financial support was meager, so sometimes he built furniture to earn money for life's essentials. He was bi-vocational, like the Apostle Paul on mission to the gentiles long before.

Something about this rugged, pioneer land stirred Warner's soul and moved him to meditate and write. A long poetic reflection on Nebraska later was published by Warner (1890). One sees in these reflections a combining of Warner's poetic sensitivity, his love of nature, sense of history, and readiness to be a courageous church reformer. He was a pioneer minister insisting on a return to biblical foundations.

Here are a few lines that might well describe what, in just a few years, would be the role Warner himself would be playing in the Christian community:

> O think ye dwellers on this beauteous land,
> How much ye owe your Maker's loving hand.
> Turn now thy mind toward the rising Sun,
> The rugged woodland coast, where first begun
> Thy sires, with hearts of iron hardihood,
> To charge upon a thousand miles of wood.
> They swung their steel in cheerful honest toil,
> And let the sun-shine on our freedom soil.

One day the intended "beauteous land" of God's church would be judged by Warner stricken by drought and decay. He would have the "heart of iron hardihood" to let new light shine on the fertile soil of committed believers who were willing to look east, to the apostolic sources of their faith.

Unfortunately, in the midst of all Warner's settling in and reflections, his journal writing either stopped temporarily or now is lost. He did write occasionally for the *Church Advocate,* the national paper of the General Eldership of the

Churches of God.[5] Significantly, on May 1, 1874, he put in his journal this observation of great concern to him: "Sectarian bigotry abounds here in the west, each sect fearing the rottenness of its own foundation and unwilling to have it tried by the gospel." He added on May 10: "Oh how the commands of God are made void by the traditions of men!" This was a significant seed of prophetic insight that would bear much reforming fruit later in his eventful ministry.

Marriage and Missionary Service

Warner also kept writing to "my darling Sarah." He was feeling both the cold winds of the Nebraska winter and the warm winds of a growing love. Having just planted four churches in February, 1874 (Fairmount, Cropsey, Evergreen, and Anderson), and now serving fourteen preaching places, he still had time to pray and dream, especially as he traveled. On March 23 he had to drive his horse and buggy thirty-five miles against a cold Nebraska wind, but his soul was warm indeed. In only a few weeks, after a year of separation, he planned a trip back to Ohio. Sarah filled his mind. "Oh, how our hearts yearn to be together! Lord, speed the time.... O Lord, what a blessing thou hast here bestowed on thy unworthy servant!... God give grace and strength of mind to endure this torture of separation."

The separation would not be long now. Marriage plans were formalizing. But first, he would have his own home in Nebraska. It was a crude little building constructed on homestead land with the help of several men. The total cost of the materials was only $32. On the evening of April 13, 1874, in damp weather and with a little stove just put in place, Warner retired for the night. It was the first night of his life that he would sleep in his own home on his own land. He was alone except for his horse, Mattie Blaze; but Sarah was prominent in his thoughts.

Warner arrived back in Upper Sandusky, Ohio, on May 23. The marriage day for Sarah and Daniel was set for June 4, a day on which "I was early out to breathe the balmy air....

Sarah (Keller) Warner

Never have I heard the birds sing so sweet and melodious as this morn, in the woods over the way from Father Keller's brick farmer's home." A Brother Burchard performed the marriage ceremony in the afternoon. It was a wonderful day. The groom was in his early thirties and the bride not yet out of her teens. They were committed to Christ and were willing to return together to the rigors of the Nebraska frontier. They would be companions in the Lord's service, whatever the cost.

The new couple left for the West on August 11, an emotional departure especially for Sarah, nineteen, untraveled, and already pregnant. John Morrison imagines the scene this way: "As their train pulled out of Chicago and plunged toward the great West, the coach's open windows gulped in the hot and cinder-laden air. By the time they crossed the great Mississippi River, Sarah's fair skin was darkened with soot and sticky with sweat. But even so, in Daniel's eyes she looked all the part of the sweet angel that she was" (Aug. 25, 1974, 9). They both loved the Lord with all their hearts and intended to face every struggle together.

The Warners were greeted in Nebraska by swarms of grasshoppers and news of a drought and major crop failure. Things did not look good. At first Sarah joined Daniel on most of the buggy rides between his many preaching points in five different counties. But soon winter approached, Sarah's pregnancy developed, and so did their anxiety about adequate housing. Constantly staying with others in different houses as they traveled would not do for much longer. Daniel's little house, set up the previous spring, would never do for a wife and baby. His credit was not established locally so that he could buy lumber for building something better, so they sent a request to Sarah's parents, asking for a loan.

The Kellers back in Ohio chose not to extend a housing loan. As it turned out, this refusal hardly meant that the Kellers had turned their backs on the pioneering couple. It probably meant that they preferred that the baby be born in the more civilized surroundings of Ohio. Regardless, one day during the winter, when Warner went to Seward for a load of coal, he found two barrels of apples at the train depot. They had been sent to the Warners by the Kellers. It was a sincere gesture of concern. Unfortunately, Warner couldn't pay the freight charge, had to sell one barrel, and, finding the apples in the other barrel frozen, had to make apple butter from them.

"Oh God," wrote Warner in his journal, "my heart is bruised and crushed!" Then a Brother Green near Seward took sympathy on them and offered a room in his home. They had a place now, tiny, but at least something other than the shack over in Polk County. In this one room they set up their first home.

Through the winter Sarah often worried as Daniel was gone days at a time on church assignments. Warner himself struggled with priorities. "O God, must I tear myself away from the dear wife bathed in tears? But 'tis the cause of Christ and I must go. O Lord, comfort her loving heart." She hoped and prayed that he and his loyal horse were not lost in one of many prairie blizzards at below zero temperatures. They were not. In fact, Daniel helped establish the first eldership of the Churches of God in Nebraska (convened at Crete on November 7, 1874). He also had an extended public debate with an Adventist minister and clashed theologically with several "Campbellites." His heart was warm, his mind alert, and his mouth ready to advance the cause of truth as he saw it.

On March 18, 1875, a healthy baby girl joined Daniel and Sarah in the one crowded room. They named their new baby Levilla Modest. Sarah was exhausted from the birth, so Daniel quickly learned to be more domestic. He canceled a few preaching engagements, a ministry curtailment painful for him, went to the doctor for medicine, and cared for his little home and its needy occupants. Reads his journal entry of March 20: "Great weakness of back from stooping continually over the bed taking care of dear wife and babe."

Home to Ohio

Soon friends helped the Warners move back to the claim in Polk County where they hoped to build a decent house during the summer. But Warner's preaching schedule was distracting and there still was no money. The Churches of God Mission Board back East was slow and meager in its support and local church people had very little cash. The Warner's total income for 1874–75 was $301.30.

Emotions ran high. On Pentecost Sunday in 1875, with wife and baby well and many scattered believers giving encouragement if not much dollar support, Warner's grateful soul prompted many lines of poetic praise in his journal. "Thank God," he wrote, "for a beautiful day. All nature seems to be awakening from the long winter slumber to praise God."

But increasingly it also was a painful time. Warner recorded in his journal (Sept. 12, 1875) that Father and Mother Keller "have no sympathy for us here on the frontier.... Many have grown cold. Brothers H— and O— would not go to meeting. Went on to the Bense Schoolhouse. Preaching time, but no one there. O Lord, the waves are rolling over me!" So, as fall approached, with the threat of another unbearable winter soon to follow, the Warners did the only practical thing. To the delight of the Kellers, little Levilla and her parents moved back to Ohio. Driven by necessity to abandon this mission field, there was a sense of relief, frustration, and failure, especially on Daniel's part.

Warning signals were on the horizon. Daniel had returned to Ohio a discouraged man. The lack of money, the harsh conditions, health threats to a new baby, the stance of the Kellers, and the persistent homesickness of Sarah had joined to force leaving Nebraska. The marriage of Sarah and Daniel, seemingly so ideal, was subtly under growing pressure. That fall the Warner's were ministering in the Ashland Circuit of Ohio. The Nebraska years had been ones of heroism and heartbreak. More of both lay just ahead.

One can hardly avoid the striking similarity between Warner's Nebraska experience and that of John Wesley earlier. Wesley also went through a period of religious questioning and near despondency following a difficult and failed missionary experience to the Indians, in this case in the American colony of Georgia (1735–37). In the process Wesley was influenced significantly by Moravians, spiritual descendants of the German Pietist movement who sought to raise the level of spirituality in the Lutheran church. Daniel Warner was nurtured by writers like John Winebrenner who brought Pietist insights to bear on a staid denomination also of German origin. For both Wesley and Warner, what lay just beyond the deep waters of near despair was the richness of sanctifying grace that would lead to amazing ministries designed to shatter the deadness of nominal Christianity. Now Warner had a theological heritage that gave him vision. Soon he would gain the holiness context that would propel it forward into action.

Questions for Group Discussion

1. Are our religious beliefs really our own, or are they mostly reflections of what others have shaped for us? How did John Winebrenner influence Daniel Warner? How should Christians "pick a church"?

2. Have you ever wondered what happened to the Eldership of the Churches of God (Winebrennerian) that so impressed and shaped Warner? Might there be a congregation of this body in your area today? Is there a bridge that could be built even now on the basis of this common heritage?

3. Warner also was involved in preparing for the launching of an educational institution of higher learning, now known as the University of Findlay (Ohio). How should faith and reason be related? How important is formal education to the preparation of Christian leaders?

4. Are the private lives of Christian leaders ever really private? Should they be? How can commitment to the work of Christ be pursued without neglecting duty to one's own family? Can grief be channeled into new life?

5. Early in his ministry, Daniel Warner became sensitized by his observation of "the seed of sectarian bigotry." Give examples of what this meant. Does it still exist?

6. How should Christians support missionaries that they send to difficult places so that such committed people can focus on ministry without tragic consequences to their own private lives?

Notes

1. Andrew Byers recalled this time in Warner's life and interpreted it this way: "To join a sectarian denomination is never by divine prompting, but is urged from human source. A young convert possessing the spirit of Christ is naturally at home in the Lord and with Christians anywhere.... Accordingly, our young brother was only 'acting natural' when he manifested no particular anxiety to 'join the church' " (1921, 51).

2. See C. H. Forney (1914), Richard Kern (1974), and Harvey Gossard (1986).

3. See *Church Advocate* 35:51, 2, and Cummins (1974).

4. A transcription of this handwritten journal was done in 1972 and resides in the archives of Anderson University. One copy is footnoted and carries explanatory notes prepared by Kenneth Lee Watts.

5. A bibliography has been developed of all articles by or news notices about D. S. Warner in the *Church Advocate* over the years (available in the Anderson University archives). From volumes 32 to 42, some 100 entries appear.

Daniel S. Warner's Ministerial Activities

Delivered his first sermon	Easter 1867
Licensed by the West Ohio Eldership (Winebrennerian)	October 1867
First pastoral assignment, Mount Blanchard, Ohio	October 1867
Pastorates held, revivals conducted, Ohio	1867–1873
Wrote for Church Advocate (Winebrennerian)	1868–1877
Elected First Clerk, West Ohio Eldership	October 1870
Founded, pastored a congregation in his hometown, New Washington, Ohio	1871–1873
Home missionary in Nebraska	1873–1875
Helped establish first eldership in Nebraska	November 1874
Pastor, "Ashland, Ohio, Circuit"	fall 1875
Resigned pastorate in Canton, Ohio, area to become a full-time holiness evangelist	November 1877
Ministerial license revoked by West Ohio Eldership	January 1878
Received "new commission" joining holiness and all truth	January 1878
Recognized as minister by the Northern Indiana Eldership	February 1879
Joint editor, *Herald of Gospel Freedom*	February 1879
Published first book, *Bible Proofs of a Second Work of Grace*	1880
Addressed Western Union Holiness Convention	December 1880
Editor of the new *Gospel Trumpet*	1881–1895
Elected Adjutant-General, Salvation Army	April 1881
Traveled with his "flying ministry" team	1886–1891
Ministered two and one-half months in Southern California	1892

Professing and Publishing Holiness
(1877–1880)

In many ways the years 1877 and 1878 were the most crucial in Daniel Warner's life. The death of his mother on July 13, 1876, had been something of a watershed, a symbol of changing times. Leah represented his past and, although not herself a Christian until the last six years of her life, she had played a key role in first bringing Daniel to faith. Her life of seventy-one years was full of "trouble and care," but, "sorely tried [her] patience never was exhausted." Warner reported in his journal his deep gratitude for his mother: "Thy pure life was my only star of hope.... Praise the Lord for a good and holy mother!" (July 18, 1876). In October 1870, Daniel was privileged to baptize his mother in the St. Joseph River. She then had associated with the Churches of God congregation at South Bridgewater, Ohio, joining her son in a life of active faith.

Sarah and little Levilla now were Warner's family. He had more in common with Sarah's parents, the Kellers, than with his own father who soon would die an unbeliever (June 1878). Daniel and Sarah had a small house in Hayesville, Ohio, close to the Keller's. Daniel was able to arrange the credit necessary to buy a pump organ for the home. Sarah loved to play hymns on it for her husband and child. The eldership then moved the Warners to the Shenandoah Circuit, which included the town of Vermillion. There, in midst of pastoral duties and evangelistic engagements, Warner enrolled in Vermillion College. In fact, in the summer of 1877 he and Sarah set up housekeeping in a college-owned home near the campus. Daniel studied, preached, and wrote doctrinal articles for the *Church Advocate,* the national paper of the Churches of God.

Outwardly at least, ministry was fulfilling and the general circumstances of life had stabilized. Warner was appreciated by the eldership. A Rev. Ober from Texas assisted Warner in a meeting at Mansfield, Ohio, in the fall of 1876. Afterward, he reported that "D. S. Warner is a model young man, of deep piety and superior courage and means business in the work of the ministry, and if he continues he will make his mark in the church." A report given by the Nebraska Eldership Standing Committee in 1877 said that "the Churches of God at Wayland and Pleasant Hill have suffered greatly on account of the resignation of D. S. Warner two years ago." At about this same time the West Ohio Eldership expressed its belief that an institution of higher learning was needed to support the church's work. A committee was appointed to seek this desired end. Warner was one of its three members.[1]

Inwardly, however, Warner was more than an active and respected church leader. He was still on a spiritual journey. His ongoing pursuit of God's highest provision and intention for himself and the whole church would bring dramatic change for his family and many others in the years ahead.

Embracing Holiness Teaching

The major dynamic stimulating this coming change in Warner's life was Christian holiness. He was not aware at the time that a generation of leaders of the holiness movement in the United States had just died[2] and that a new generation was about to emerge. It would, and he would be a key member of the new group.

In 1877 Warner came into close and, for a change, positive

contact with holiness people. At first this contact featured the spiritual experiences of his own wife and her parents. The Kellers first became involved with holiness people in Upper Sandusky, Ohio. When Daniel, Sarah, and Levilla visited the Keller farm in April 1877, Daniel immediately sensed that something was different. His in-laws always had been good Christian people, but now he noticed that "this whole family has recently made a more full consecration to God and realized an increased experience of holy joy." He observed that now "God's presence still more pervades the happy household of sanctified children of God."

The keys to true holiness were thought by Warner to be thorough human consecration, a pervasive divine presence, and resulting joy known individually and in the body of believers. He was curious, open, spiritually hungry, but had to be convinced. In 1880, while addressing the Western Holiness Convention in Illinois (see Appendix C), he recalled:

When I went to the first holiness meeting I ever attended, what do you think I expected? I thought they would work themselves up into a high state of feeling, and get their seekers so wrought up also, that they would finally get to the point of a physical sanctification. But I really found them, each with a Bible in his hand. They were so much one that I could not tell who was the leader of the meeting. And they all searched the word.

Daniel and Sarah went to some of the holiness meetings in Upper Sandusky. On April 8 Sarah went forward to the altar and claimed her own "sanctification." Daniel was pleased, supportive, and yet still cautious. He already thought of himself as committed to Christ and already obedient to the Spirit. He certainly had sought to be disciplined in his faith and faithful with his gifts. Was there really more? The holiness workers said there was a "second work of grace." Members of his own family now professed such a work and their lives witnessed to its meaningfulness. They told him that he also needed to be sanctified.

Warner was a spiritual seeker. He already had been an evangelistic preacher for ten years, witnessing hundreds of conversions to Christ in meetings that he had conducted. Nonetheless, he remained active in restudying the Bible for fresh understanding of subjects like holiness. Despite his earlier opposition to holiness teaching and practice, at least the kind he had observed firsthand, he now was questing for a deeper walk with God, a more victorious way, an experience of being utterly sold out to God. His prayer was that he be filled with the wonderful Spirit of the Lord.

On April 16, 1877, he noted in his journal: "Since I rose this morning my constant prayer has been to God to lead me in all things. I pray God to take me like an old sack and shake me until entirely empty, and then fill me with the fullness of God." The search continued. On July 5 Warner was leading a holiness meeting in Mansfield, Ohio. After a time of Bible reading and congregational testimonies, he issued the usual invitation, then himself stepped down to the altar to seek sanctification. His spiritual life was not yet satisfying. Now, very publicly, he was seeking more of God's transforming grace for himself.

That very evening another service was in progress in the same place. When the time came, he did as in the morning, kneeling at his own meeting's altar. He reported later in his journal that "all was dark" and he felt "ashamed to bow at the altar and seek sanctification of 'soul, body, and spirit' after I had invited sinners to, and labored with them, at the same altar." Pride can be a real problem, especially for a respected public leader. The next morning he read 1 Peter 5:10, "But the God of all grace, who hath called us unto his eternal glory in Christ Jesus, after that ye have suffered a while, make you perfect, stablish, strengthen, settle you" (KJV). He so hoped that God somehow would perfect, settle, and establish him. Then he read Ephesians 3:14, 16–19. There it was! He had only to accept the Spirit's work by faith.

Fill Me with Thy Spirit, Lord

" . . . be filled with the Spirit."—Ephesians 5:18b

7.7.7.7.wR.
FILL ME

Daniel S. Warner

Andrew L. Byers

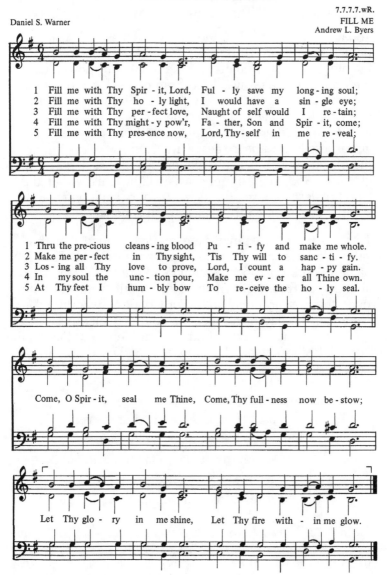

1 Fill me with Thy Spir - it, Lord, Ful - ly save my long - ing soul;
2 Fill me with Thy ho - ly light, I would have a sin - gle eye;
3 Fill me with Thy per - fect love, Naught of self would I re - tain;
4 Fill me with Thy might - y pow'r, Fa - ther, Son and Spir - it, come;
5 Fill me with Thy pres-ence now, Lord, Thy-self in me re - veal;

1 Thru the pre-cious cleans-ing blood Pu - ri - fy and make me whole.
2 Make me per - fect in Thy sight, 'Tis Thy will to sanc - ti - fy.
3 Los - ing all Thy love to prove, Lord, I count a hap - py gain.
4 In my soul the unc - tion pour, Make me ev - er all Thine own.
5 At Thy feet I hum - bly bow To re - ceive the ho - ly seal.

Come, O Spir - it, seal me Thine, Come, Thy full - ness now be - stow;

Let Thy glo - ry in me shine, Let Thy fire with - in me glow.

His journal entry of July 7 is pivotal. From this day on, his life and ministry would be different. What his soul yearned for now had been found! The testimony of this day reads in part:

Today we fasted all day. Met in the Bethel at 9 A.M. and held meeting until after 4 P.M. without intermission. Evening, met at a quarter to eight. Mighty power filled the house. The altar was filled from one side to the other. Several were seeking sanctification. Glory to God, this night he [God] began to give me some of the evidences (besides my hitherto naked faith) that I had got out of the wilderness into Canaan. Jesus, my blessed Savior, just cut me off one bunch of the sweet grapes of this "land." Oh, glory to God, once more I was a little child! I felt the blood of Jesus flowing through my entire soul, body, and spirit. Heaven on earth! Hallelujah, it is done!

This testimony to sanctifying grace is much like that of Charles Wesley's witness to his experience on May 21, 1738. That historic day had been a Sunday, Pentecost Day, the day of the Upper Room gift of the Holy Spirit from the Father, through the Son, to the church. For Charles it was "the day of deliverance, the day of his life: the day for which he will borrow the experience of Peter in the jail of Herod, or Paul in the prison at Philippi, and the language of David, Isaiah, and Jesus Christ.

> Long my imprisoned spirit lay,
> Fast bound in sin and nature's night.
> Thine eye diffused a quick'ning ray.
> I woke; the dungeon flamed with light!
> My chains fell off, my heart was free;
> I rose, went forth, and followed Thee.[3]

From July 7, 1877, to his last day of life in 1895, Daniel Warner was a committed holiness evangelist and writer. By July 28, two weeks after the sacred cleansing and empowering, he already had written two articles on holiness for the

Church Advocate and was anxious to cooperate with the National Holiness Association. Shortly he would begin work on his first major book, *Bible Proofs of the Second Work of Grace* (1880). The focus of his ministry had shifted, and this shift soon would bring change in his thinking and church relationships.

About a month after his experience of holiness, Warner sat under the teaching of Daniel Steele, a prominent holiness advocate, and began filling his journal and personal library with books and references to a range of holiness works. Warner now fed on such literature. Then he heard a Brother Rice, a Methodist minister, preach a sermon on sanctification, only to learn that this preacher had just had his ministerial license taken away by the Northwest Ohio Conference of that denomination. The reason was that Rice was preaching holiness (presumably he was thought to be a divisive voice in the tradition of the Wesleys, a tradition that had been born in holiness preaching!).[4] Harold Phillips ponders: "One cannot help wondering, did he [Warner] have intimations of what might lie in store for him at the same type of intersection between ecclesiastical control vs. felt conviction?" (Sept. 22, 1974, 8).

Intolerable Denominational Restrictions

Warner's new enthusiasm for this doctrine of sanctification soon brought increased tension into his relationship with the West Ohio Eldership. A warning signal had appeared as early as April 1876. Warner was pulled into a church "trial" conducted by the eldership. A Rev. McNutt was being brought to account for trying to establish a new congregation in Upper Sandusky, a town not supposed to be in his assigned ministerial territory. McNutt asked Warner to speak on his behalf. The minister bringing the charges turned out to be Joseph Neil, the very minister who had officiated at the wedding of Daniel Warner and Tamzen Kerr in 1867.

Warner was shocked at such a proceeding. A good man, with good evangelistic intent, was under attack by his own church. McNutt's character was smeared publically, and he collapsed and had to be carried out of the trial room. Daniel was visibly shaken. Such bitter rivalry between ministers! How could one justify the evil of oppressive church organizations that could act this way?

In September 1877, the showdown started. It began at Blooming Grove, Ohio, where Warner was holding meetings with an old friend, William Oliver. Oliver was suspicious of Warner's holiness work. On September 16 Warner preached the morning sermon on 1 Corinthians 13, stressing the need for "perfect love" brought by the Holy Spirit. Oliver interrupted the sermon, denouncing the "theory" of sanctification.

It took some minutes for Warner to be able to proceed. Things were tense. That evening Oliver assumed the preaching role and used the chance, with Warner sitting in a pew, to ridicule the holiness movement. After the service Oliver approached Warner, handed him a folded document, and walked away.

Thinking that this document was a list of prayer requests, Warner did not read it until later that evening. Rather than requests for prayer, it was the beginning of the end of Warner's connection with the General Eldership! It read, with Warner's responses to three of the four charges, as found in his journal:

The following charges are preferred against Elder D. S. Warner:

First, for inviting a sect of fanatics calling themselves the Holy Alliance Band to hold meetings in the local Churches of God without consulting the Elders or trustees or myself. [Warner: Thank God that calling people hard names does not make them such, but only shows the depravity of the accuser. No band was invited, but simply persons from different localities who enjoyed holiness.]

Second, for joining in with this said band and bidding them Godspeed and thereby has brought schism and division among those churches. [Warner: The charge of schism is without the least shadow of foundation. Through the mercy of God a few souls have been sanctified from their pride, etc., and qualified to be useful in the church.]

Third, for the accommodation of this professed holy band that he invited to hold a meeting of ten days in the Church of God chapel in Mansfield, Elder D. S. Warner did on the evening of the 8th of July in less than one hour have the ordinances of washing the saints' feet and the Lord's supper attended to.[5] [Warner's response is not available.]

Fourth, for stating publicly in Shenandoah about the 26th of August that he had been preaching his own doctrine prior to seeking his so-called holiness. [Warner: This is a mistake. I simply said that on sanctification I used to preach what I believed, but now I am able to testify that I know.]

—W. H. Oliver

These charges soon were heard by the West Ohio Eldership in formal session. They were sustained despite the fact that Rev. Oliver finally admitted writing himself some "letters" of opposition to Warner that first were said to have been written and sent by churches on Warner's circuit. Warner's ministerial license, nonetheless, was renewed, but only on condition that he not again bring such holiness workers into any congregation of the denomination without advance permission of the elders. Valuing his church connection, he reluctantly agreed to this restriction and was assigned to a circuit in the Canton, Ohio, area.

One should not judge too quickly Oliver's motive and method in bringing the charges or that of the eldership in its restriction of Warner's ministry of holiness. What can be said with confidence is that they and Warner were coming to represent two different perspectives. The Churches of God leaders were cautious, conservative, oriented to the stability of their religious establishment. Warner had abandoned himself to holiness, was prepared to experiment, risk, and launch out for God regardless of institutional implications. He was the leading edge of a new tendency in the larger holiness move-

ment to "come out" of whatever human structures and traditions impeded the free flow of God's Spirit. When traditional
lines are crossed freely, of course, there is a fine line between
being "pushed out" and "coming out." Howard Snyder (1980)
has documented a movement later in John Wesley's life
toward the "charismatic" in ways similar to the experience of
Warner. For Wesley this movement finally resulted in a separation of the "Methodists" from the Anglican Church. Says
Franklin Littell of Wesley:

> Throughout his active life he shifted by steady steps from
> the developmental and sacramental view of the institu-
> tions of Christendom to normative use of the New
> Testament and reference to the Early Church. He justified
> field preaching and the itineracy, class meetings and their
> disciplinary structure, and finally the ordination of minis-
> ters for America, on the argument that he was following
> "apostolic" practice. He became, in his basic orientation,
> a Free Churchman (1961, 113).

By November 1877, despite his church's restriction on his
ministry, Warner felt strongly impressed by God to become
active as a full-time holiness evangelist. So he resigned his
appointment, he and Sarah sold their organ and featherbed to
raise some money, and they moved to the home of Sarah's
parents, the Kellers, near Upper Sandusky. While not his
direct intent, he now was on a collision course with the eldership.

The next month trouble really began. Warner was conducting a revival in Findlay, Ohio. For the first two nights the
meeting was hosted voluntarily by the local Church of God
congregation. Then, because of developing resistance there,
services were moved to the city courthouse. The Church of
God pastor in Findlay, J. V. Updike, supportive of a holiness
emphasis, reported in the January 9, 1878 issue of the
Church Advocate:

> The Lord is working in Findlay, praise his holy name.
> Yesterday I baptized 6. Up to this time 22 have made the

good profession. A part of them are backsliders, but all needed all they got; 20 professed the blessing of entire sanctification. Oh, that all would seek this glorious work! Pray for us.

—J. V. Updike

In the January 16 issue Warner reported similarly on this meeting, adding that Brother Updike himself had been "sanctified through the blood of the Lamb."

A complaint reached the West Ohio Eldership. Action came quickly. Charles Brown observes: "Now Warner was to experience one of the bitterest disappointments of life to have this small group [Winebrennerian Churches of God], for whom he had sacrificed so much, turn upon him and rend him with hostility, only because he had taken a further step on that road of sheer idealism which had brought him to them in the first place" (1951, 68).[6]

On January 30, 1878, Warner was brought to trial by his church. So was Rev. Updike, who apologized for being too cooperative with the Ohio Holiness Alliance and thus was only reprimanded. Updike did defend his own holiness experience as biblical but promised to be more cautious about future involvement with traveling holiness preachers. He was given a probationary license. Warner, however, was not apologetic about open cooperation with the holiness movement.

The charges brought against Warner this time were as follows: (1) transcending the restrictions of the eldership; (2) violating rules of cooperation; and (3) participating in dividing the church. The concern was that Warner had been drawn into a parachurch euphoria of emotionally charged and unauthorized meetings that were drawing people and resources away from a reasoned faith and the established churches.[7] Warner, of course, viewed the concern and his resulting dismissal quite differently. He insisted that he had been disfellowshipped "for preaching full salvation, for following the Holy Spirit, and for helping to save over 150 souls [in Findlay]." Following an article by Warner in the *Church Advocate* titled "Answer to Questions on Sanctification" (42:41), this footnote was added by the editor: "No more articles will be published by D. S. Warner since his connection to the Eldership is ceased."

Time often brings a more balanced wisdom. Removed from the emotional setting of frontier revivalism, the crucial topic of sanctification has been reconsidered both by the Churches of God (Winebrennerian) and the Church of God movement that evolved in part from Warner's ministry and writings. There now appears to be more agreement than disagreement between these bodies on this topic. Compare the section "Sanctification" in Churches of God: General Conference (1986) and Kenneth Jones (1985).

A New Commission

There is a fine line between torchbearer and troublemaker, prophet and pest, conserver of the past and freedom from the past for the sake of the future. The next day, having learned of the eldership's final decision in his case, Warner's feelings were strong and mixed. He was brought to the train depot in a sled because heavy snow was falling. Once on the train, he encountered Brother Cassel, one of the committee members who had just rendered the judgment against him. Warner wrote in his journal that evening (Jan. 31, 1878):

> I thanked him for their decision and assured him that if I were to look upon the matter from a mere human viewpoint and consider my attachment to the Church of God and her principals, I would regard their action a dreadful calamity and intolerable to bear, but that I had now that charity that "believeth all things" and "endureth all things," and therefore I calmly rested in the promise of God that "all things work together for good to me" and the sweet assurance that my dear Father to whom I belonged would turn this and everything else (as long as I stay on the altar) to my good and his glory. Praise his holy name....

Now Warner was affiliated only with the Holiness Alliance

in Ohio. He began to reflect on the implications of the holiness teaching for the unity of all Christians. Clearly he viewed his own ministry as uniting and not dividing. His journal reads regarding the charge of dividing the church: "I showed that the only results of the holiness meeting were fifty-three sinners converted and 118 believers sanctified, and that all the division and confusion was caused by the carnal and wicked opposition on the part of the rest of the church, just like the envious Jews stirred up the people at Thessalonica and Berea (Acts 17) and interrupted the apostles in their peaceable work of leading souls to Jesus.... The apostles, of course, had to bear the blame, and ... bonds and prisons awaited them; and I, too, was ready to suffer affliction with the people of God for the sake of Christ" (Jan. 30, 1878).

Holiness is healing, not rupturing. In fact, holiness now was seen as key to true Christian unity. The crisis faced when Warner was rejected by a denominational establishment led him to a new commission for his own ministry. This key entry appears in his journal for March 7, 1878: "On the 31st of last January the Lord showed me that holiness could never prosper upon sectarian soil encumbered by human creeds and party names, and he gave me a new commission to join holiness and all truth together and build up the apostolic church of the living God. Praise his name! I will obey him."

For the rest of his life Daniel Warner would never pastor again, but always be an itinerant evangelist, writer, and editor. He would be an unapologetic and relentless advocate for the holiness of Christians, a liberating holiness that should enable a divinely inspired unity among Christians. He would place special stress on such matters as "the unity of believers in Christ, the reality of a victorious Christian life cleansed and empowered by the presence of the Holy Spirit, [and] the kingdom of God as a present spiritual reality with Christ as its King (Phillips, Oct. 20, 1974, 7).

This "new commission" related primarily to his own ministry as an active holiness evangelist, not yet to some new "movement." Warner was not aware that his insights were coming to be shared by many others in scattered places. A clear movement consciousness would not evolve until the 1890s, with others even then more responsible for promoting it than Warner was.[8] For now he knew that he must somehow get on with his new commission.

The challenge of this great task was to begin with a time of deep personal sorrow. Mountain tops tend to lead to nearby valleys. Daniel's seventy-five year old father died on June 16, 1878, at his home near Bryan, Ohio, after a long illness. David resisted faith in Christ to the very end. While waiting with his brothers Joseph and Lewis for the funeral, Daniel received a most upsetting telegram. His little daughter was seriously ill back on the Keller's farm where she and Sarah were staying. He rushed home and within days his beloved Levilla, age three, was dead of meningitis.

The funeral for Levilla was on June 25, Warner's thirty-sixth birthday. His journal includes a moving account of his own memory of the little girl's adorable characteristics, her tragic illness, death, and funeral, along with a poem express-ing a father's grief and faith (see Appendix D). By September Warner himself was seriously ill with "bilious remittent fever and an attack of hemorrhage of the lungs." He took to his bed in early October. His doctor was alarmed, fearing for Daniel's life, but God still had much for him to do. He was active again by late October, although bodily frailty persisted as a lifelong problem.

With sanctifying grace to motivate and sustain, Warner seemed to grow stronger in the face of all this illness and death. "As a giant oak grows strong in the fierce winter wind, he grew to spiritual greatness through unceasing battles and storms" (Brown 1951, 68). He was an opportunist and over-comer for God. On one of his frequent trips in the summer of 1878, for instance, he and Sarah were caught in a runaway-horse accident. Sarah was rushed to a nearby farm for some emergency care. The neighbors arrived to check on all the excitement. Warner reports: "A small congregation gathered and I preached a short discourse, of course on holiness."

Temporary New Arrangements

Being forced to leave the West Ohio Eldership was painful indeed. Daniel Warner was a strong individual, but he was not an independent who was pleased to be on his own in the Lord's work. He loved the church, needed the church, cared deeply that all of God's people accept and strengthen each other in holiness and unity. Now that his ties with the General Eldership were broken, not by his own doing, he sought some fellowship in which there would be mutual accountability and, of course, where he could be free to proclaim holiness.

Some evangelistic meetings in Indiana brought him into contact with a suitable body, the Northern Indiana Eldership of the Churches of God. This was a separated branch of the same church from which he had been expelled. It had broken fellowship with the Indiana Eldership in 1877, primarily over the issue of secret societies. The particular society in question was Freemasonry. Many Indiana ministers and their congregations had withdrawn and formed the new eldership, in part in protest against the unquestioning acceptance of Masons as Christians.

Although still recovering from his illness, Warner made a special effort to attend this new Eldership's annual meeting. It was held at the Churches of God grounds at Beaver Dam, Indiana, in October 1878. There he was accepted into the young fellowship as a recognized minister. After the first day's proceedings Warner wrote this in his journal: "The manner in which business was done and the good degree of devotional spirit with which it was pervaded was a great stride from the carnal and formal wranglings of Elderships of the present to the simplicity and spirituality of an apostolic Eldership. Praise God, he is leading his children out into the glorious freedom of the gospel."

Part of this glorious freedom, as Warner saw it, was an action taken in relation to the group's new publishing effort, the *Herald of Gospel Freedom*. The *Herald* was a four-page periodical published by this eldership in Wolcottville, Indiana, since January 1878 (subscription was fifty cents a year). I. W. Lowman, a leader in the new eldership's formation, was editor. The decision now was to enlarge the paper, issuing it semimonthly and devoting a part of it to the promotion of Bible holiness. Warner could see "glorious results from this project. It is bringing about what the Lord showed me last winter; that is, a people straight before God in holiness and truth." He now viewed holiness as "the great lever of power" that since the Protestant Reformation had been "weakened and encumbered by party names and creeds and human traditions."

Lowman and the eldership turned to Warner for help. The editing responsibility (and privilege) Warner received was to edit a new holiness section of the *Herald*. For several years Warner had written articles for the *Church Advocate,* the publication of the General Eldership of the Churches of God. Lowman thus knew of Warner and respected his work. Now there began "a connection with editing and publishing which was to throw this relatively unknown preacher of holiness [Warner] into the very center of what later became a great religious movement" (J. Smith, 1965, 8). Lowman and Warner prepared a 1879 prospectus for the paper, a position statement declaring that the church truly is God's (see Appendix B).

The Warners moved to Rome City, Indiana, in November. The operations of the *Herald of Gospel Freedom* also moved there in February 1879. By March Warner had bought half interest in the paper for $250 and joined I. W. Lowman as joint editor and publisher. He then became the paper's editor in 1880 and soon was seeking to ensure its financial stability and further expand its influence by consolidating it with some other holiness publication. Warner now was an evangelist, editor, and publishing entrepreneur.

For the time being Warner sensed that he was well situated to pursue his calling. He was active in opposing sectarianism and upholding his new commission that featured holiness as an alternative to rampant church division. He now had a dual church affiliation, the Northern Indiana Eldership and the

National Holiness Association.[9] Both were supportive of his holiness emphasis and at least the former was in direct sympathy with his anti-sectarianism.

Warner also had developed a congenial relationship with a segment of the Mennonite community in northern Indiana, the Evangelical United Mennonites of Goshen. He even promoted a proposal to merge the Northern Indiana Eldership and the United Mennonite Church (see Appendix F, also G for a more contemporary statement). Increasingly he was concerned about church organizations that wielded power, licensed and reprimanded preachers, and claimed the leadership of the Holy Spirit while appearing to exercise tight and often self-serving control of church life. To him it seemed that there should be more openness within church bodies, more toleration of ministry views, closer cooperation with like-minded Christians in other bodies. He was prepared to risk and experiment with ways to remove walls that tend to obstruct the Spirit's work among all believers.

Although this proposed merger never happened for whatever reason,[10] Warner continued working closely with these Mennonites. They took a strong stand for holiness as a possible and necessary experience for every believer following justification.[11] It was natural, then, that Warner's substantial volume *Bible Proofs of the Second Work of Grace,*[12] was published in 1880 in Goshen, Indiana, by the Evangelical United Mennonite Publishing Society. It was the first book released by an author representing what would be the Church of God movement (Anderson, Ind). This pivotal book keynoted much yet to come. Warner began his lengthy and passionate writing with this:

> After that the kindness and love of God our Savior appeared unto me in removing the veil of ignorance and deep prejudice from my heart; enabling me to see and appropriate Christ as my sanctification, all the longing of my heart seemed to center in a desire that all God's dear children should enter this "valley of blessing so sweet".... The church is God's appointed means of saving the

world. But perfect holiness is her normal condition.... Having ... perceived that this "second grace" is the ultimate end of Christ's death, and the great burden of the apostolic ministry, I was constrained to dedicate, for ever unto the Lord, all the energies of my being for the promotion of this great salvation (1880, 7–9).

Questions for Group Discussion

1. The experience of sanctification became vital to Daniel Warner's whole ministry. Has an emphasis on holiness lessened in today's church life because of our secularized setting? How might this loss be reversed?

2. History is more than a mere recounting of what happened in the past. It also is an interpretation by the historian. How should we account for the version of Warner's separation from the Ohio Eldership recorded by that body's historian? He refers to Warner rather negatively as "the leader in Ohio and westward of a body of people who gave the brotherhood considerable trouble" (Forney 561).

3. Is it always the way of organizations, including churches, to resist change, to restrict whatever might upset the comfortable status quo? How can a body of Christian people be properly disciplined without restricting the work of the Holy Spirit in the process?

4. What was Warner's "new commission"? Is it still an important mandate for the church today? Is your congregation doing anything to implement such a commission?

5. Warner tried early in his ministry to achieve a greater degree of Christian unity through a "church merger." Is it appropriate today to experiment with fresh ways to further the unity goal? What would be one good possibility in your own community? How helpful are the recent guidelines found in Appendix G?

Notes

1. Findlay College (now the University of Findlay in Findlay, Ohio) actually was founded in 1882 when Warner no longer was associated with the eldership. See Richard Kern (1984).

2. Alexander Campbell, the "restorationist" leader, died in 1866 just as Warner was beginning his Christian life. Now the holiness leaders Phoebe Palmer and Charles Finney died, 1874 and 1875 respectively.

3. As quoted by T. Chrichton Mitchell, in *Charles Wesley: Man with the Dancing Heart* (Kansas City: Beacon Hill Press, 1994), p. 64.

4. In 1860 Benjamin Roberts, also a vigorous holiness advocate who was forced out of the Methodist Episcopal Church, founded the Free Methodist Church. For a comparison of the Free Methodist Church and the Church of God movement just prior to the twentieth century, see Barry Callen (1969, chap. 3).

5. Apparently one concern was that an inordinate focus on Christian "experience" inevitably brings a casual attitude to the administration of the ordinances (participating in them quickly as though they are of minor importance).

6. Note the Barry Callen masters thesis (1969) that focuses on the theme of idealism and the Church of God movement that Warner's experience and ministry helped spawn. Callen says: "The pioneers of the Church of God Movement ... found themselves insisting that no Christian ought to be satisfied until the ultimate implications of the Christian faith had been actualized in the life of the church. Thus, they lifted their eyes to the possibilities of grace; they opened themselves to the invited invasion of 'all truth'; they refused to recognize the validity of organizational and creedal obstacles awkwardly erected between brothers [and sisters] in Christ; in short, they gave their utmost for God's highest. This was their 'ecumenical ideal' and they cried out for its actualization" (5).

7. Earlier, Alexander Campbell of the Disciples tradition

also had been very critical of the emotionalism of camp meeting revivalism. Even Warner at first had denounced it as "fanaticism." Much earlier John Wesley found a middle path between deep spiritual experience and uncontrolled and unaccountable "enthusiasms" (see Ferrel Lowell, "John Wesley and the Enthusiasts" in *Wesleyan Theological Journal* (spring/fall, 1988), pp. 180–187.

8. See John Smith (1980), chapter five.

9. This organization, known initially as the National Campmeeting Association for the Promotion of Holiness, was first formed in Vineland, New Jersey, in July 1867. Soon regional and state affiliate organizations began to form. The national body continues today as the Christian Holiness Association. The *Wesleyan Theological Journal,* scholarly publication of its theological arm, the Wesleyan Theological Society, currently is edited by Barry Callen of the Church of God movement.

10. This particular Mennonite body was formed in 1879 by the merger of the Evangelical Mennonites and the United Mennonites. It existed with this name only until 1883 when it joined with the Brethren in Christ to become what today is known as the Missionary Church. Its available records only mention Warner's proposal of a merger with the Northern Indiana Eldership of the Churches of God and the appointment of a representative to explore the matter further (see *Gospel Banner,* October 1879).

11. See Article XII, "Of Sanctification," in *Doctrines and Discipline of the Evangelical United Mennonites* (Goshen, Ind: E. U. Mennonite Publishing Society, 1880), 20–21.

12. This hardback book had 493 pages and sold for $1.25 per copy.

The Year of Decision
(1881)

Participants in the early Wesleyan/Holiness Movement apparently were avid readers. Holiness papers were common, sometimes competitive, and often ceased publication altogether or merged with others. For example, the official paper of the Church of the Nazarene, *Herald of Holiness,* was established as this denomination's official organ in 1912, but its history stretches back into Warner's time. Four papers lay behind this one, and "each of these had at least two direct ancestors."[1] A similar pattern is seen in the earliest editorial work of Daniel Warner.

The first issue of the *Gospel Trumpet* appeared January 1, 1881. It originated from Rome City, Indiana, and was a merging of *The Pilgrim,* published in Indianapolis by G. Haines, and the *Herald of Gospel Freedom.* Warner was founding editor, with publishing supervision provided by the Northern Indiana Eldership of the Churches of God. Warner's subsequent ministry would be felt by the world largely through the medium of this new holiness paper. Although he did not know it at the time, he was "standing on the threshold of an exciting adventure for both himself and the whole Christian church" (J. Smith, 1965, 9).

The new paper carried this statement of purpose: "The glory of God in the salvation of men from all sin, and the union of all saints upon the Bible." Expressed here were the major burdens of Warner. He had been "disillusioned with the shortcomings of the denominational system of his time—the fierce and unbrotherly rivalries, the rigidity of creedal systems, the lack of any real and deep commitment to serious Christian living on the part of so many nominal church members. With Bible in heart and hand, and by faith, Warner saw something better than this" (Phillips 1979, 21).

Only two issues of the new *Gospel Trumpet* were published in Rome City. Haines owned a job-printing business in Indianapolis, the state's rapidly growing capital city, so he suggested moving the *Trumpet* there. This seemed a progressive idea. In February 1881, this holiness periodical found a home at 70 North Illinois Street, Indianapolis, very close to the railroad station and the new state house then under construction. This was an exhilarating setting, certainly different for Daniel and Sarah whose backgrounds were in small farming communities. Maybe now the publishing of holiness would move more to center stage in the mainstream of public life.

By the summer of 1881 the Haines-Warner partnership had dissolved. Warner paid Haines $100 for his share of this obviously modest operation. The negotiation led to the reluctant agreement of Haines not to launch a rival holiness paper in Indianapolis. He soon did, however, even sending samples of his new paper to *Gospel Trumpet* subscribers.

Warner wrote of this awkward circumstance. He deplored such a development as necessarily hurtful to the holiness cause. Haines is said to have brought to the previous partnership "a chilling iceberg, an austere, worldly, complaining, and mere money policy." Warner notes that the primary time commitment of Haines had been to his other role as Indianapolis agent for the *Cincinnati Times-Star*.[2] Already beginning was what has been called "the miracle of survival,"[3] a miracle that would have to last for years. Publishing the holiness message, especially in opposition to the denominational establishments, was hardly a lucrative or persecution-free business. It required very dedicated and sacrificial servants. Daniel Warner surely was one of these.

Warner managed on his own the best he could. He moved the printing office to his own home at 625 West Vermont Street and built a makeshift office beside the house using lumber from an old horse stable that he tore down himself. There he began printing the paper, setting all type and doing all the folding and addressing by hand—and by himself at first. There were only a few hundred subscribers to serve in this tedious way. When winter came, the drafty little office was not at all practical and there was no money to plaster the walls so that

Early *Gospel Trumpet* masthead

the cold could be kept out. There seemed only one option. He moved the noisy and ill-smelling printing press into the kitchen of their home, reporting that "Dear Wife tendered her kitchen to the Lord for the use of publishing salvation. Praise the Lord!"

Sarah Warner had just given birth to their second child, son Sidney. There they were, with little money, a new baby, a press in the kitchen, and few people who seemed to care. About the only bright spot was a subscriber in Michigan, a

Joseph Fisher who was so enthusiastic about the *Gospel Trumpet* that he sent generous support and voluntarily sold subscriptions. Soon Warner was listing Fisher on the masthead as the co-publisher.

As the issues of the *Trumpet* kept coming, in spite of all obstacles, a conviction of Warner's kept growing. Back in 1868, near the very beginning of his ministry, Warner had purchased a copy of the book *Discourses on the Nature of Faith* by William Starr (1857). Starr was a Congregational minister in Illinois who felt his ministry stifled by a restrictive church establishment. Sometime before 1880, Warner wrote this annotation in his personal copy, alongside Starr's call for believers to rise up against sectarianism and bring to reality a "holy and unified church" (Starr 231):

> If this holy man, perceiving only the eavil [*sic*] of division is thus moved to cry out, what must be the guilt of one who sees both the eavil [*sic*] and remedy and yet will close his mouth and see the world go to ruin?

I'm Coming Out!

By 1880 Daniel Warner himself was ready to cry out and act out against sectarianism. An increasing number of leaders of the holiness movement were feeling significant tension between their passion for church renewal and the viability of their continuance in their home denominations. Soon there would be new holiness-oriented denominations, one way of finally dealing with the holiness movement's "search for order" (Dieter 236–275). Another way was that of the more "radical" holiness reformers who soon became known as "come-out-ers." Prominent among them was Daniel Warner.[4]

Daniel Warner now was growing impatient with compromises to his vision. His "new commission" carried major implications that, at least in his judgment, could not be ignored any longer. Like a growing number of others, he "sought to apply the logic of Christian perfectionism, with all its ultraistic inclinations of the perfectionist mentality, to the church question"

(Dieter 246). The first compromise that Warner called into serious question was his own participation in the Holiness Association. By doing so, he was "the first to propose such radical applications of the revival's promise of unity among all true Christian believers" (246).

Both his affinity with and his questioning of this association can be seen in one setting in 1880. A convention of the Western Union Holiness Association convened from December 15–19 in the Brooklyn Methodist Episcopal Church in Jacksonville, Illinois.[5] The planning committee said that this gathering of about two hundred holiness leaders from a range of denominations and states would only be in the interests of holiness. Thus, it was to be "strictly and purely undenominational." People were to come not representing any particular denomination, but only to celebrate and strengthen "the holiness cause."

One delegate was to represent each holiness periodical, with all delegates to be in agreement with the doctrine of holiness "that sets forth entire sanctification as an instantaneous work of God, wrought in the heart through faith, subsequent to conversion." Likely Daniel Warner was present both as a representative of the *Herald of Gospel Freedom* and because he had been asked to make a formal address, an honor in this select ecumenical crowd. He also was appointed to the program committee charged with the responsibility of planning the next convention.

The topic of Warner's address to the convention was "The Kind of Power Needed to Carry the Holiness Work." The main point he made was that "it is the power of God Himself that is needed for this work." He warned that "the devil is set against this work.... We need God's power to the fullest degree promised to meet this adversary." "God is looking around to find someone he can trust," announced Warner. God "generally finds them among the holy ones." (See the complete text of this address in Appendix C).

Some of the statements by other speakers heard by Warner at this convention stirred a struggle within him. For instance,

Thomas Doty from Cleveland, Ohio, editor of the *Christian Harvester,* said that "if you belong to a church, it is your duty to promote holiness right in it: in the Presbyterian church, as a Presbyterian; in the Baptist church, as a Baptist, etc." Doty admitted that he disliked the whole denominational idea, but said God "permits it, and so must we." Warner did not address this issue in his formal remarks, but M. L. Haney (Methodist Episcopal) did. He attacked come-outers "who insist on the silly dogma of no-churchism, and favor the disorganization of all Christian forces."

It may be that, as Warner heard these men speak this way, "the conviction was being cemented in his heart and mind that there was no room for him and for the burning message he felt in a situation where denominationalism was being exalted and continued membership in a denomination being made a requirement of continued fellowship and acceptance" (Phillips, Oct. 20, 1974, 8). The message beginning to burn inside Warner tended to question the easy, status-quo assumption that God passively permits rampant division of Christ's body, the church. Maybe being a "come-outer" was the way to go. Warner saw the charge of no-churchism as very wrong, unfair, and demeaning of the unifying potential of the promised sanctifying power of the Spirit. He believed deeply in the church and refused to accept the claim that genuine reliance on the Holy Spirit to establish and guide the church inevitably was the way of anarchy. Is God the author of confusion? The church is, after all, God's church!

The strength of Warner's convictions grew and began to be acted out. In April, 1881, he was elected Adjutant-General in the Salvation Army in Indianapolis. He promised that the *Gospel Trumpet* would carry reports of some "battles and conquests of the Lord's Salvation Army." But the February 8, 1882, issue reported an apparent end of this relationship. Being joined to anything but the Lord now was said to be a trick of Satan.

This vigorous view rooted in an event in April 1881. While conducting a revival meeting in Hardinsburg, Indiana, Warner "saw the church." No longer would he be patient with church bodies that organized their lives on the basis of sect recognition and requirements. For years Warner had been troubled about the inconsistency of his repudiating "sects" in principle and yet continuing to belong to organizations that insisted on basing their memberships on formal sect recognition. Now he no longer would condone the disjunction between his holiness-generated unity vision and the standard acceptance of sect division.

Instead, he would be faithful to a fresh vision, a new way of conceiving how things might be. The Israelites of the Exodus and the Babylonian Exile finally were able to see dramatic new possibilities in the worst of circumstances. Their seeing opened their imaginations, inspired their faith, and generated new hope. Warner now walked this ancient prophetic path. As Merle Strege puts it, Warner rejected "the American religious status quo, the business-as-usual way of denominational religion" (1993, 96). Since it really is God's church, surely there is a better way.

This position brought an immediate crisis in Warner's relationship with the National Holiness Association.[6] "The Spirit showed me," he wrote, "the inconsistency of repudiating sects and yet belonging to an association that is based on sect recognition."[7] No longer would he be patient with the placing of human conditions on membership in God's church. He went to a meeting of the association in Terre Haute, Indiana, in May 1881 and tried to get changed the "sect endorsing clause" of the association so that its membership would be open "to all true Christians everywhere" (whether denominational adherents or not). The effort failed. So he reported in the *Gospel Trumpet* on June 1: "We wish to co-operate with all Christians, as such, in saving souls—but forever withdraw from all organisms that uphold and endorse sects and denominations in the body of Christ."

The stance of the Holiness Movement did not generate for itself the dilemma faced by Warner. Its purpose was to be a transdenominational renewal force. Its primary concern was not the evil of denominationalism as such, although some leaders were uncomfortable by all the formalized division, but the evil of nominal Christianity. The intent was that participants in the holiness associations would remain loyal members in their respective denominations so that they could be renewed by the holiness emphasis and return to their denominational homes to broaden the renewal impact. The extent of Warner's renewal vision was greater than this, thus the inevitable clash.[8]

Reported church historian Henry Wickersham in 1900: "Before this he [Warner] was in good standing with many editors and sectarian holiness workers, but because of his decided stand for the truth, he was denounced in their papers, set at naught by the ministry, and rejected by his former friends" (300). According to sociologist Val Clear (1977, 36):

It was in the small cells of the holiness-minded individuals scattered about the country in the 1870s and 1880s that the future adherents of Warner's movement were to be found. Most of the holiness people stayed within their denominations, forming a type of church-within-the-church. But many others were disaffected, felt that Old Ship Zion was sure to sink. For many of these latter persons, D. S. Warner became a spokesman, and the *Gospel Trumpet* was his voice.

The significance of Warner is clear. In this earliest phase of the life of the Church of God movement, "it was Warner who was prophet, teacher, evangelizer, poet, advisor, theologian—the voice of the reformation. Since the *Gospel Trumpet* was the only formal organizational entity, it was Warner's dominant personality and the *Trumpet* that kept the movement from disintegrating into a thousand isolated and disconnected parts" (Reardon 24). So far as the larger holiness movement is concerned, Warner is the one who brought to the movement clear elements of the Anabaptist tradition, in part from his reliance on the teachings of John Winebrenner and his close association with the Evangelical United Mennonites in northern Indiana.[9]

Having ruptured his formal tie to the holiness movement, Warner wasted no time in reviewing his future with the

Northern Indiana Eldership of the Churches of God. In October 1881, he attended a meeting of the eldership in Beaver Dam, Indiana. There Warner tried and again failed to gain acceptance for the radical implications of his holiness-unity vision. He proposed that this body "conform more perfectly to the Bible standard with reference to government" by

Church building near Beaver Dam where in October 1881, Warner and 5 others declared their freedom from sectarian Christianity.

ending the practice of granting ministerial licenses and eliminating formal church membership procedures so that all who bore the fruit of true regeneration would belong automatically by the action of God. When this body said a firm no, five people walked out of the meeting with Warner, declaring that they were "coming out" of all sectism. Thus was constituted in Beaver Dam the first congregation of the Church of God movement.

This walk-out was repeated later in the same month in Carson City, Michigan. Joseph and Allie Fisher, staunch

My Soul Is Satisfied

"I pray that out of his glorious riches he may strengthen you with power through his Spirit in your inner being."—Ephesians 3:16

Daniel S. Warner

MY SOUL IS SATISFIED
Barney E. Warren

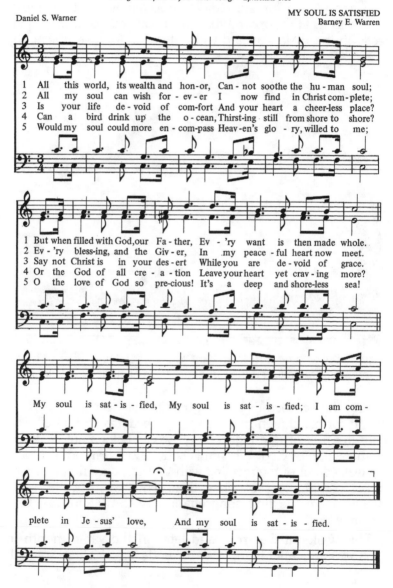

1 All this world, its wealth and hon-or, Can - not soothe the hu - man soul;
2 All my soul can wish for - ev - er I now find in Christ com - plete;
3 Is your life de - void of com-fort And your heart a cheer-less place?
4 Can a bird drink up the o - cean, Thirst-ing still from shore to shore?
5 Would my soul could more en - com-pass Heav-en's glo - ry, willed to me;

1 But when filled with God, our Fa - ther, Ev - 'ry want is then made whole.
2 Ev - 'ry bless-ing, and the Giv - er, In my peace - ful heart now meet.
3 Say not Christ is in your des - ert While you are de - void of grace.
4 Or the God of all cre - a - tion Leave your heart yet crav - ing more?
5 O the love of God so pre-cious! It's a deep and shore-less sea!

My soul is sat - is - fied, My soul is sat - is - fied; I am com -

plete in Je - sus' love, And my soul is sat - is - fied.

Trumpet supporters, had asked Warner to come to Michigan to speak to a special holiness meeting being held prior to the annual camp meeting of the Northern Michigan Eldership, also a breakaway from the General Eldership over issues like Freemasonary. The local congregation objected to the holiness meeting, so the Fishers and twenty others, finding this the last straw, left the eldership.

So a second group had separated from sectarianism. The "Carson City Resolutions" to which they agreed include this: "That we adhere to no body or organization but the church of God, bought by the blood of Christ, organized by the Holy Spirit, and governed by the Bible.... That we recognize and fellowship, as members with us in the one body of Christ, all truly regenerated and sincere saints who worship God in all the light they possess, and that we urge all the dear children of God to forsake the snares and yokes of human parties and stand alone in the 'one fold' of Christ upon the Bible, and in the unity of the Spirit" (see Callen, 1979, I, 295–96).

Here were elements of the rationale for a new movement, one intending to be truly transdenominational. Joined were the passion for Christian holiness, the dream of Christian unity, and the belief that the first enables the second only when free of the artificial restrictions of human attempts to organize and run the church.

Warner's thrust was echoed by John Morrison as he addressed the 1963 International Convention of the Church of God convened in Anderson, Indiana. He told the crowd of thousands that "Christian fellowship ought to be wide enough and warm enough to take in a Christian wherever you may find him." Then he concluded:

So go home loving all Christians; but for heaven's sake don't join any of them! That's right! As I understand it, D. S. Warner's major contention was that a person can be a good Christian and cooperate with other Christians in proper fashion without joining any of the religious organizations known as churches. You do not join the Church—you are born into it! (see Callen, 1979, II, 651).

The Reformation Glory

"There is one body and one Spirit—just as you were called—one Lord, one faith, one baptism; one God and Father of all, who is over all and through all and in all."—Ephesians 4:4-6

Charles W. Naylor

REFORMATION GLORY
Andrew L. Byers

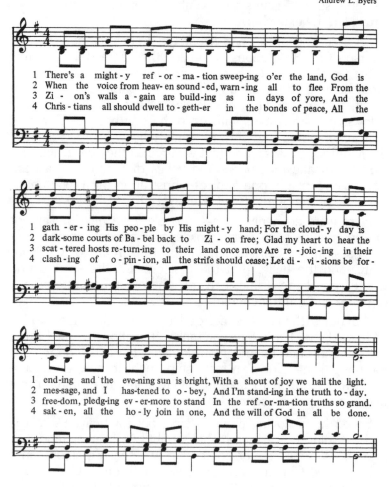

1 There's a might-y ref-or-ma-tion sweep-ing o'er the land, God is gath-er-ing His peo-ple by His might-y hand; For the cloud-y day is end-ing and the eve-ning sun is bright, With a shout of joy we hail the light.

2 When the voice from heav-en sound-ed, warn-ing all to flee From the dark-some courts of Ba-bel back to Zi-on free; Glad my heart to hear the mes-sage, and I has-tened to o-bey, And I'm stand-ing in the truth to-day.

3 Zi-on's walls a-gain are build-ing as in days of yore, And the scat-tered hosts re-turn-ing to their land once more Are re-joic-ing in their free-dom, pledg-ing ev-er-more to stand In the ref-or-ma-tion truths so grand.

4 Chris-tians all should dwell to-geth-er in the bonds of peace, All the clash-ing of o-pin-ion, all the strife should cease; Let di-vi-sions be for-sak-en, all the ho-ly join in one, And the will of God in all be done.

O the ref - or - ma - tion glo - ry! Let it
O the ref - or - ma - tion glo - ry, O the glo - ry!

shine to ev- 'ry land. We will tell the
Let it shine to ev- 'ry land. We will tell the

bless-ed sto - ry; In its truth we e'er shall stand.
bless-ed sto - ry, bless-ed sto - ry;

A new "movement" now was gaining momentum and definition with the Beaver Dam and Carson City events. The
Gospel Trumpet was its primary medium of conveyance, with
Warner its tireless visionary and mouthpiece. The purpose of
this holiness paper changed because of the dramatic events of

1881. Before then the *Gospel Trumpet* had been one of many holiness papers; but after Beaver Dam and Carson City, it became Warner's major vehicle for furthering his cause.

This cause drew considerable sympathy from many Christians longing for more vision and power, more holiness and unity than they had found to date. Judges Melvin Dieter (256): "Warner's promise of a group, gathered together under the guidance and instruction of the sanctifying Spirit, free of denominational and sectarian trammels, as he pictured them, combined with a reformatory, eschatological thrust, carried a certain populist magnetism."

Most holiness people who separated from their denominations during the last quarter of the nineteenth century thought of themselves as "pushed-outers," not "come-outers." They judged themselves chased off by the increasing "carnality" in the churches, a sin situation intolerant of a holiness renewal.[10] Warner was both pushed out (West Ohio Eldership) and later intentionally came out of the Holiness Association and the Northern Indiana and Northern Michigan Elderships. In all instances, holiness was the key issue. At first, holiness was an unwelcome emphasis. Then holiness generated a unifying vision that called believers out of the compromised and unresponsive denominations.

The Last Reformation

Warner would devote the remaining fourteen years of his life to restoring the unity of God's people through the sanctifying work of the Holy Spirit. He was a "come-outer." He and soon many others "saw the church," a vision of the seamless, undivided body of Christ. Warner began sprinkling the pages of the *Gospel Trumpet* with testimonies of fresh sightings of the church beyond division.[11]

The "perfect love" of sanctification, it was argued, enables Christians to live above sin, including the sin of rending the body of Christ. Human lines of denomination, race, sex, and social status are to be discounted, even ignored in the face of the transforming grace of God in Christ. The emphasis should be on seeing, not arrogantly claiming to be the whole, pure, undivided church. The vision calls for refusing either to erect or recognize human controls on Christian fellowship. God sets the members in the church. It's God's church!

Warner finally had found a church home. It was the whole body of Christ. He sensed God moving to complete the sixteenth century Protestant Reformation and the eighteenth century Wesleyan revival in a "last reformation." There was a new sense of liberty and joy, inspiring Warner to compose many new songs that express the fresh vision. As one song by Warner and B. E. Warren testifies: "My soul is satisfied; my soul is satisfied; I am complete in Jesus' love, and my soul is satisfied." Another announced, "There's music in my soul."

So strongly did Warner feel about the new movement that he later renumbered the volumes of the *Gospel Trumpet*, repudiating its first three volumes when it had appeared under earlier names and in connection with the Northern Indiana Eldership of the Churches of God. He explained his action this way:

> Since the *Herald* was started back in the fogs of Babylon, and died before it saw the evening light clearly, we have desired to drop off its three years and cast it back into the burning city where it belonged, and have our volume indicate the actual number of years that the *Trumpet* has been sounding. For when a person gets clean out of Babylon, that should be the beginning of months and years to him.[12]

Historian John Smith summarizes Warner's experience this way:

> He had found the freedom in Christ for which he had so long sought. A new ingredient entered his life. It was as if he had been released from a great load and for the first time was able to stand erect. He felt as though he had stepped from the condemnatory shadow of his own and all other sectarian walls and now stood in the full light of

truth—the 'evening' light of which the prophet Zechariah had spoken. There was indeed cause for rejoicing. God had begun a new work in the church (July 25, 1965, 8).

These breaks from traditionally organized Christian denominations focused on (1) rejecting all sects, (2) refusing to form another, (3) in part by not defining or limiting the new cause by any set creed. The emerging movement was similar to many previous movements by its (1) seeing the church as a voluntary gathering of all and only the truly regenerate (like the Anabaptists, Campbellites, etc.) and (2) highlighting the Bible and the Spirit as together the sufficient guides to all truth (Quakers, etc.). The distinguishing feature of this new "cause" was primarily that Warner and others "put all of these emphases in a single package and then wedded them to the Wesleyan doctrine of holiness" (J. Smith, 1980, 48).[13]

The early tone of this new cause was aggressive indeed. In the new year's greeting for January 1882, the *Gospel Trumpet*, that is, editor Daniel Warner, was very plain:

> To Babylon and all her concomitants, we promise nothing but fire, sword and hammer, and confounding blasts from the armory of God's Word. We have scarcely begun the bombardment of the wicked harlot city. By the grace of God, we expect to deal with sin and sinners as we never yet have done.... We know no man after the flesh, and we seek to please no man.

Several editors of other holiness papers, themselves now targets, reacted with criticism of this new stand that claimed to be outside the presumed evils of sectism. Warner sought to answer them at length.[14] The new freedom had its own dilemmas—and certainly its detractors (soon even to include Mrs. Warner!). It still does. It also has its vision, its hope, its determination to release the church back into God's control.

Questions for Group Discussion

1. How can one account for unethical behavior (such apparently as that of Haines) going on in the name of Christian holiness? Is hypocrisy and the waywardness of Christian leaders a problem in today's church?

2. How easily we forget the past sacrifices of others who, at considerable cost to themselves, provided present benefits for many of us. What were the first elements of the "miracle of survival" as Daniel Warner sought to keep a young publishing ministry alive?

3. What was the basic difference between the views of Warner and those of the National Holiness Association on the issue of "come-outism"? From what today should the church come out?

4. What do you understand the phrase "seeing the church" to have meant to Warner? Do you share such a vision? Should there be human conditions placed on membership in God's church?

5. Warner sought for years to find the right "church home." Finally he was satisfied that he had found it. What church did he choose?

6. The cause or movement that evolved around Warner's vision and convictions was characterized by what "distinguishing feature"?

Notes

1. Paul Bassett, in *Wesleyan Theological Journal* (spring/fall, 1993), 104.

2. Editorial, *Gospel Trumpet*, June 1, 1881.

3. See the history of the Gospel Trumpet Company (Warner Press) by this title, Phillips (1979).

4. Others were John P. Brooks, leader of a movement in Missouri that became the Church of God (Holiness) and James Washburn, leader of the Southern California and Arizona Holiness Association from which the Holiness Church was organized. See Melvin Dieter, "Primitivism in the American Holiness Tradition," *Wesleyan Theological Journal* 30:1 (spring 1995).

5. See the published Proceedings (1881) now housed in the archives of Anderson University.

6. Warner's specific involvement focused primarily in the Indiana Holiness Association, which at one point named him as a vice-president (Dieter 255). He also had significant contact with the larger holiness movement in both Ohio and Illinois.

7. *Gospel Trumpet*, June 1, 1881.

8. In 1993 Barry Callen, a contemporary leader of the Church of God movement, became editor of the *Wesleyan Theological Journal*, current publication of the holiness body from which Warner withdrew more than a century earlier. A sect-endorsing clause no longer is required by this holiness body. Warner's vision is admired in principle by today's Christian Holiness Association, but it still is not actively pursued as such. The primary agenda remains more the Christianizing of Christianity by in-depth renewal through the holiness experience and the holy life.

9. Says Melvin Dieter (254): Warner's "development of the church as the dwelling place of the Spirit, the baptism of believers only, the centrality of the Word of God in the midst of the congregation as the 'universal law,' the strong sense of mission as a reformer, the strongly apocalyptical tone, and even the retention of the rite of foot washing as an ordinance of the church--all may be closely identified with the Anabaptist tradition."

10. See Paul Bassett, *Wesleyan Theological Journal* (Spring/Fall, 1993), 74. A good example is the formation of the Free Methodist Church in 1860 following the experience of Rev. B. T. Roberts being "pushed out" of the Methodist

Episcopal Church. See L. R. Marston, *From Age to Age a Living Witness* (1960) and Clarence Zahniser, *Earnest Christian: Life and Works of Benjamin Titus Roberts* (1957).

11. For examples, see Barry Callen (1979, I, 123–240). See Charles Brown, *The Church Beyond Division* (1939).

12. *Gospel Trumpet*, August 1, 1889.

13. Also see John Smith's 1954 doctoral dissertation "The Approach of the Church of God (Anderson, Ind.) and Comparable Groups to the Problem of Christian Unity."

14. See the *Gospel Trumpet,* Jan. 16, 1882. Also see Byers, 1921, 299ff.

Writings of Daniel S. Warner

1880 *Bible Proofs of the Second Work of Grace.* Goshen, Ind,: E. U. Mennonite Publishing Society.

1885 *Songs of Victory.* Joseph Fischer, Ed, Warner major contributor of original material. Williamston, MI: Gospel Trumpet Co.

1888 *Anthems from the Throne.* With Barney Warren. Grand Junction, Mich: Gospel Trumpet Co.

1893 *Echoes From Glory.* With Barney Warren. Grand Junction, Mich.: Gospel Trumpet Co.

1890 *Poems of Grace and Truth.* Grand Junction, MI: Gospel Trumpet Co.

n.d. *The Church of God or What Is the Church and What Is Not.* n.p.

1894 *The Sabbath or Which Day to Keep.* Grand Junction, MI: Gospel Trumpet Co.

1896 *Innocence: A Poem Giving a Description of the Author's Experience from Innocence into Sin,* and *From Sin to Full Salvation.* Grand Junction, Mich: Gospel Trumpet Publishing Co.

1896 *Salvation: Present, Perfect, Now or Never.* Moundsville, WVa: Gospel Trumpet Co.

1897 *Marriage and Divorce.* Grand Junction, Mich: Gospel Trumpet Co.

1903 *The Cleansing of the Sanctuary.* With Herbert Riggle. Moundsville, WV: Gospel Trumpet Co.

1972 *Journal of D. S. Warner.* Unpublished, reprint from the original. Large portions reproduced in Andrew Byers, *Birth of a Reformation* (1921). Handwritten original now in the Archives of Anderson University.

There are numerous poems, hymn lyrics, journal entries by Warner, many as cited within this volume. In addition, there are scores of articles, editorials, and reports from the field in the *Church Advocate, Herald of Gospel Freedom,* and *Gospel Trumpet.*

7

Valiant for the Truth
(1882–1893)

Difficulties quickly arose to obstruct the joy of Daniel Warner's new vision of a church united in sanctifying grace. Leading God's people into a new freedom always comes at a price. During Warner's lifetime, for instance, the *Gospel Trumpet* publishing operation moved six times, involving three different states. It formed in Rome City and then went to Indianapolis, Indiana, shifting later to Cardington (1882) and Bucyrus, Ohio (1883), then on to Williamston (1884) and finally Grand Junction, Michigan (1886).[1] These moves always were efforts to take advantage of apparent opportunities to better the fragile financial situation of the modest-scale publishing work.

Risk and stress always were involved. There were numerous obstacles, not all financial. Warner was assaulted personally by the enemies of divorce, defection, and death. But through all transition and persecution, he remained valiant for the truth.

Hell Recoiled in Fury Black

Warner's early publishing partner in Indianapolis (Haines) had withdrawn and started a rival paper. Another trusted partner (Fisher) soon would divorce his wife so he could remarry, precipitating another crisis. There were several other such unethical or immoral agendas that Warner had to face along the way. At times there also was vigorous, sometimes irrational, sometimes even violent opposition. He and his associates reported often to the *Gospel Trumpet* that they had been threatened, beaten, shot at, and run out of some town. These reports "read like a nineteenth-century version of the Book of Acts" (Allison, Jan. 5, 1975, 15).

One example happened in November, 1883. Warner called for the first "general assembly" of the "saints" to meet in Annapolis, Ohio. It was to be a great gathering for the preaching of holiness and healing. The invitation read, "Come, ye who are in bondage of sect captivity, and learn your way out of the wilderness" (Byers, 1921, 289).

Some people, obviously not saints, arrived with other purposes in mind. An L. H. Johnson of Toledo was opposed to holiness and harangued the services from the back of a wagon. Three other men were opposed to the wearing of collars, lace, and eyeglasses. Warner rebuked them as fanatics when they stretched out on the floor and tried to disrupt Warner's sermon by moaning aloud. A meeting that Warner expected to be "a sample of the reign of heaven" was later described as "Satan loosed."

In July 1887 a similar thing happened at a meeting being conducted near St. James, Missouri, along the Meramec River.[2] Some people got the "jerks." Their hollering, twisting, and speaking in tongues were, they mockingly said, manifestations of the Holy Spirit. Warner rebuked the obvious and intentional excesses, read aloud 1 Corinthians 12–14, and "showed the beautiful harmony of the Church under the control of the Spirit of God, that 'love does not behave itself unseemly.' "[3] Things finally settled down, but trouble was not over in this place.

Some local denominational leaders apparently were most displeased at the big crowds and the anti-sectarian flavor of this revival. Late one night a masked mob rode up with sticks and rocks and violently drove the evangelists away. They especially wanted Warner, but he had escaped into the night. In the days to follow, despite the opposition, cottage meetings continued, with reports of many conversions and healings.

A poem Warner published in the December 15, 1883, *Gospel Trumpet* reflects the anguish he experienced over the sin of his own early life and now "the pains of hell" having to be endured in the process of being faithful to God's call. In part it reads:

> I ought to love my Savior;
> He loved me long ago,
> Looked on my soul with favor,
> When deep in guilt and woe:
> And though my sin had grieved him,
> His Father's law had crossed,
> Love drew him down from heaven
> To seek and save the lost.

> I ought to love my Savior;
> He bore my sin and shame;
> From glory to the manger
> On wings of love he came:
> He trod this earth in sorrow,
> Endured the pains of hell,
> That I should not be banished,
> But in his glory dwell.[4]

The first appearance of this hymn poem in 1883 was in these additional negative circumstances in Bucyrus, Ohio: "Cold weather, a cold office, and the departure of our main printer have caused the long delay of this issue. Having finally purchased and improved the office, we hope to go forward again. Pray on."

The biggest personal trial was yet ahead. It would be "undoubtedly the greatest emotional shock of his [Warner's] entire life" (J. Smith, July 25, 1965, 8). An R. S. Stockwell

identified himself with Warner and began assisting in the publishing work when it was in Bucyrus, Ohio. Soon, however,
Stockwell started advocating a new definition of holy living.
Sexual relations were said to be carnal, even in marriage. To
be "entirely" sanctified, he insisted, is to express the kind of
love that can be shared with all the saints. Sarah Warner listened carefully to this "third work of grace" teaching and soon
came to agree. Her husband did not.

Then in January 1884, Stockwell increased the pressure on
Daniel Warner. He announced that God had revealed to him
that Warner should sell the publishing work and that there was
a man ready to buy. Probably tiring of all the stress involved
and no longer believing in the anti-sectarian message carried
by the *Gospel Trumpet,* Sarah joined actively in wanting
Daniel to sell out. She, Stockwell, and others pressed Warner
to give in, but he could not. He remained sure that the paper,
with its cause of Christian holiness and unity, was still God's
will for him. So Stockwell left, and so did Sarah! She returned
to her parents in Upper Sandusky, temporarily taking along
their son, Sidney. It was the beginning of the end for the
Warner marriage.

Warner hired a housekeeper for the winter, found a new
financial backer in Williamston, Michigan, and planned to
move the company again. The backer was a Thomas Horton
who came to Bucyrus, Ohio, paid all the debts of the paper,
chartered a railroad car, and saw to the moving to better facilities of all the printing equipment and the gospel workers. In
the move of the publishing work to Michigan in 1884, "lovely
Sadie" (Sarah) did not go along. Instead, she denounced her
husband and his "come-outism" in a public letter published at
her request in the *Christian Harvester* (May 1, 1884).

In this published letter, Sarah Warner claimed to possess
"perfect salvation in Jesus." She said that her eyes now were
opened "to see the evils of come-outism." "I am free from it,"
she announced, "and forever renounce it and praise God that
he has so completely delivered me from the spirit of it. I am
thoroughly convinced that this effort to unite God's people by
calling them out of the churches is not God's plan of unity. It

simply cuts off a few members by themselves, who get an idea that none are clearly sanctified unless they see as 'we' do; and, then, they have a harsh grating that is the very opposite of love."

Sarah spurned all of Daniel's attempts at reconciliation. As she continued to maintain the separation, hope faded. Finally she relinquished to Daniel the custody of their son, Sidney, in 1888, and filed for divorce in 1890 (granted in April without Daniel contesting the now inevitable). Sarah charged Daniel with being "willfully absent" from her for two years. She had abandoned him and his work and thus claimed that he had deserted her. Her heart and life now lay elsewhere. By God's

Home of Gospel Trumpet Publishing Co.
Grand Junction, MI, 1886-98.

grace, his ministry remained credible and on track despite it all.

Warner especially deplored Sarah taking their private trouble into print, so he felt it necessary to respond at length.[5] It was a personal embarrassment, of course, but worse was having two holiness papers used as vehicles for holiness advocates to attack each other.

This could be devastating to the holiness cause. In his

anguish Warner was unable to publish the *Trumpet* for four months, committed as he was to it. He did manage to compose a moving poem titled "To My Dear Sidney" (*see* Appendix D), a father's reflections addressed to his little son who was caught in the middle of this ruptured marriage.

In 1890, at the Beaver Dam, Indiana, camp meeting, Daniel would have the privilege of baptizing his nine-year-old son and then performing the wedding of two of his evangelistic team members, Barney Warren and Nannie Kigar. But the joy was bittersweet, as seen in these lines in the poem to his little son:

> A comfort left in sorrows deep,
> > One heart to beat with mine.
> Thy life has dawned in peril's day,
> > Mid wars that Heaven shake;
> Thy summers five, eventful, they
> > Like surges o'er thee break.
> Thy little soul has felt the shock,
> > Of burning babel's fall;
> When hell recoiled in fury black,
> > And stood in dread appall.[6]

The deep hurt of the personal tragedy of Sarah's divorcing him would never leave Daniel, even though some years later he would remarry after having learned of Sarah's remarriage and then death.

One of his later books (1897) explores in detail the biblical teachings on marriage and divorce.[7] This subject unfortunately had forced itself into his own life. The concluding sentence of this book reads: "The Lord give us both wisdom and love, that we may properly balance the claims of justice to the law of the Lord, and pity to the souls of men. Amen" (31). This prayer was very personal for the author and remains very relevant today!

Warner's traveling evangelistic company, 1885–89. (l to r, standing) Barney Warren, Nannie Kigar, Frances Miller (later Warner's wife). (Seated) Warner and "Mother" Sarah Smith

Working While It Is Day

Personal grief, however, could not be allowed to cripple the call and divert the cause. There was no time to brood over what could not be changed. Sarah was gone. In Williamston, Michigan, for the first time the *Gospel Trumpet* had a real home with reasonable facilities. Here the "Trumpet Family" became a reality (the group of gospel workers living communally, sharing together the work and the cause). This "family" was now the only one that Warner had until his young son rejoined him.

Probably the first camp meeting associated with the evolving new movement of the Church of God began meeting in 1883 near Bangor, Michigan, in back of a schoolhouse on the Harris farm (Confer 2). During the 1886 Bangor Campmeeting there was discussion about moving the Trumpet office to that locality. A substantial building was for sale right next to the intersection of two railroads in Grand Junction.[8] It soon was purchased for eight hundred dollars with the help of Sebastian Michels of nearby South Haven.

Time seemed short. Daniel Warner now believed that he was living in the "last days," with the return of Christ probably not many years away (although he was not a firm date setter).

A. L. Byers and family. Byers was inspired to ministry by Warner and was Warner's biographer (*Birth of a Reformation,* 1921)

The task was not strategic planning and laying foundations for lasting institutions. The good news needed trumpeting as clearly, widely, and quickly as possible—whatever the obstacles thrown up by the enemy. God was on the move among the faithful!

Only one freight car was needed to bring to Grand Junction all publishing machinery, supplies, and the household goods of the workers. So, in June, 1886, the *Gospel Trumpet* had another new home.[9] Later, in March, 1890, a house just across the street was bought by Enoch Byrum and became the residence for the whole Trumpet family (including Warner when he was not traveling). Fellowship was rich, winters harsh, and commitment to a cause strong. These were plain people outside the mainstream and often misunderstood. With rails stretching in all directions at their very doorstep, they worked sacrificially to publish and ship large quantities of songs, tracts, papers, and books.

Sometimes they played. Noah Byrum recalls that thirty-eight chickens and a garden spot came with the new house. So did a yard for the younger workers to play in.

One evening the boys got to jumping by the edge of the garden where the ground was soft and sandy. Brother Warner came along and joined the crowd as a spectator. He had not watched very long until he became so interested that he joined in the sport of high jump, standing jump, and the running broad jump. He seemed to forget his office cares as he enjoyed himself with the boys in this sport (Noah Byrum 1932, 3).

None of the Trumpet workers, including Warner, received a salary. When Sidney rejoined his father here in 1888 and wanted a little spending money, Daniel offered two possibilities. The boy would be given a few cents for every mouse he could catch in the Trumpet office building and one cent for every copy of the *Gospel Trumpet* he could sell for two cents to waiting train passengers. The intent was to satisfy a son, clean the property, and, as always, spread the word of salvation, sanctification, and the uniting of God's people.

Warner always loved the outdoors. In the summer of 1891 he and Noah Byrum went fishing at Lester Lake, a lovely rural setting about a mile north of Grand Junction just east of the railroad tracks. Warner commented that this was an ideal location for a camp meeting. It would be a reality the following year, replacing the one at Bangor and functioning to this day as Warner Camp.

Warner decided to experiment with an evangelistic technique that proved very successful. He formed a group in 1886, a touring company of gifted preachers and singers, "flying messengers" who conducted numerous revival campaigns together for four years.

The team of Daniel Warner, "Mother" Sarah Smith, Nannie Kigar, Frances Miller, and Barney Warren traveled widely in the Midwest, South, and into eastern Canada.[10] It inspired the formation of other such teams, opening the way for many gifted young leaders to get involved, including many women.

Who Will Suffer with the Savior?

"Resist him, standing firm in the faith, because you know that your brothers throughout the world are undergoing the same kind of sufferings."—I Peter 5:9

Daniel S. Warner

SUFFER WITH THE SAVIOR
Ludolph Schroeder

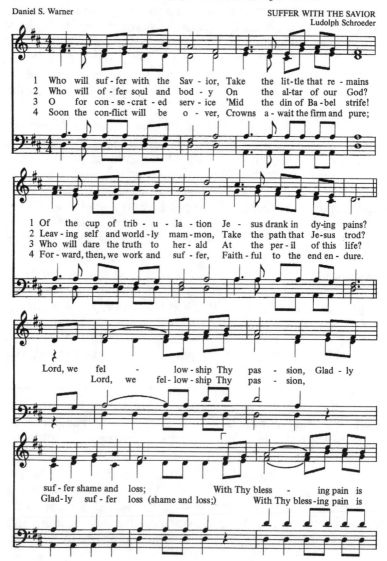

1. Who will suf-fer with the Sav - ior, Take the lit-tle that re - mains
2. Who will of-fer soul and bod - y On the al-tar of our God?
3. O for con - se -crat - ed serv - ice 'Mid the din of Ba - bel strife!
4. Soon the con-flict will be o - ver, Crowns a - wait the firm and pure;

1. Of the cup of trib - u - la - tion Je - sus drank in dy-ing pains?
2. Leav - ing self and world - ly mam - mon, Take the path that Je-sus trod?
3. Who will dare the truth to her - ald At the per - il of this life?
4. For - ward, then, we work and suf - fer, Faith - ful to the end en - dure.

Lord, we fel - low-ship Thy pas - sion, Glad - ly
Lord, we fel - low-ship Thy pas - sion,

suf - fer shame and loss; With Thy bless - ing pain is
Glad - ly suf - fer loss (shame and loss;) With Thy bless-ing pain is

116

plea - sure, We will glo - ry in Thy cross. (in Thy cross.)

Barney Warren added more than a good bass voice to Warner's quartet. Soon his skill in musical composition and harmony would be a great asset to Warner's own poetic power.

This "flying ministry" faced much opposition, yet knew much success in schoolhouses, train stations, homes, tents, churches, and brush arbors. Once Warner and Barney Warren walked the roads all night while the women in the company slept in a graveyard because a meeting had yielded no money and no home invitations. That, however, was not enough to bring discouragement.

Axchie Bolitho summarizes: "Whatever life with the Warner company may have lacked, it certainly did not lack in interest. The young people who went about with him, as indeed all who came into any close contact with the man, were constantly being astonished by fresh manifestations of the power and love of God in answer to his faith. God was very real to D. S. Warner, and he dared ask great things and attempt great things. Indeed it seemed to those about him that the atmosphere of miracle was the normal condition of Christian experience" (35).

Given the relatively frail health of Warner, it is amazing to recall that frequently he would preach two or three times in one day, with sermons often two hours in length! February and March of 1885 were spent in an evangelistic tour of Iowa and Missouri. Such tours were now the usual schedule. Alabama is one of many available examples of how tours began and worked.

Warner, son Sidney, and wife Frances

A family from the north moved into the Mount Tabor community just east of Hartselle, Alabama, and soon invited a company of preachers and singers to come down and hold a meeting. The visitors came about the middle of February 1891, and began a revival in the Methodist church that had been borrowed for the meeting. The evangelists and singers were D. S. Warner, A. L. Byers, and B. E. Warren and wife. They had large crowds. To begin with they came through curiosity, but as the meeting progressed and under the preaching and singing of the gospel many were converted.[11]

In January, 1886, Warner's group secured a United Brethren chapel and held a two-week revival in Prospect, Indiana. One night Noah Byrum, then fourteen, came with his older Brother, Eli. Noah recalled later:

The two of us arrived at the chapel an hour before it was time for the services to start, but even then almost every seat was taken.... Soon there was a commotion at the door, and someone near me whispered, "Here they come." I watched them push their way through the crowded aisles to the front of the church. Someone stepped into the pulpit. My brother leaned over and said, "That man is Warner."

Brother Warner then arose to preach. He was a striking figure, medium tall, with a long black coat and high-cut vest. He wore a full, neatly trimmed beard. He had soft blue eyes and a pleasant smile, and at once he had complete command of his listeners.... Such powerful preaching I had never heard.... For two hours the audience was held spellbound by the eloquence of that Spirit-filled man.[12]

After the large altar service that followed the sermon, Warner passed out free copies of the *Gospel Trumpet* and gathered subscriptions.

Warner remained the *Gospel Trumpet* editor, writing much, including frequent reports from the field. In addition to numerous tours made with the evangelistic company, he took long trips alone to Colorado and California. The focus always was evangelistic rather than church-planting because of the sense of urgency to get out the message and because of the bias against "organizing" the church. Warner and an increasing number of his companions were hurrying with the news, staying nowhere very long.

Later Herbert Riggle reflected on this and concluded that the lack of nurturing of new converts, patiently

Warner's son Sidney

building new congregations begun in revivals, and educating young ministers was a basic shortcoming of the movement's pioneer period (1924, 78–89). Such were not first priority tasks for Warner.

In Warner's mind and heart it seemed that first things should be first. There was a cause. The paper, guided by Warner's careful hand, had to get out the good news. According to its front-page logo, the *Gospel Trumpet* intended to be "first pure, then valiant for the truth." The truth was said to center in "the purity and unity of the church ... and the destruction of sect Babylon." "Truth," however, was not seen as a static thing to be boxed in, written down, and mastered for more use in denomination building and maintaining. Truth is Christ, salvation and freedom in relation to Christ, wholeness of the church as Christ's body.

So Warner "continued to search for a greater revelation of God's truth as long as he lived" (J. Smith, July 25, 1965, 12). He was more a pioneer than a settler.[13] He hoped to be soft clay in the Spirit's hands instead of a wall builder and church establishment protector.

Many reports of personal contact with Warner recall warm and upbuilding experiences. Andrew Byers, for instance, was only eighteen when he first encountered Warner in April 1888. Warner rejoiced with the newly converted Andrew.

And as he continued talking to me there beamed from those soft blue eyes a something which pierced my soul with an illumination which has never left me.
That he should so rejoice in spirit at the knowledge of my conversion seemed to give me a spiritual uplift and to place my appreciation of things spiritual on a higher level. It seemed that during that week when Brother Warner and company were with us our home was a heavenly paradise. Their singing seemed to carry me away. It was so different. And it fired me up for a lifelong engagement in song composition (Byers, 1921, 473). Other such testimonies are recorded with gratitude (Byers, 1921, 456–472).

Warner home in Grand Junction, MI (unrestored)

Restored Warner home on grounds of Warner Camp, Michigan

Even so, Warner's warmth could erupt as full-blown fire. He was a cause-oriented crusader for Christ intending nothing less than the "destruction of sect Babylon." He was confrontational and full of conviction. As he announced liberation in Christ from all human bondages, some people experienced him at least implying a new bondage to his own strong viewpoints. Charles Naylor, for instance, shortly before his death in 1950, said that Warner "vigorously condemned and bitterly attacked all those who did not agree with him even in matters of little importance" (Phillips, June 9, 1974, 7). Whether or not this judgment is wholly fair, there is the dilemma of rallying people around the cause of no more sectism in the church while inevitably facing the danger of that very cause functioning in a sectarian manner, intended or not.[14]

Warner recognized this apparent paradox and wrestled with it this way:

> On the authority of God's word we affirm that it is the privilege and solemn duty of all God's messengers to understand and teach the word of God in perfect harmony. This does not, however, imply that they all have the same gifts or abilities, nor yet that they have all attained unto the same degree of knowledge in sacred truth; but "whereunto we have attained we walk by the same rule," and what we have not learned of the Lord we do not presume to teach. Hence there is harmony in all that is taught, so long as each teacher is confined within that measure of truth received by the Holy Spirit.[15]

Warner was convictional, but not creedal. He was strong for the truth, but, at least in principle, ready to admit that neither he nor anyone else was ever in full possession of it. To know the truth, one must be in Christ and always on journey with Christ on behalf of God's current agenda for the church in the world.

Often profound truth and rich Christian experience get expressed better in poetry and song than in rational formulas and creeds. Warner was a visionary and poet as well as a preacher and editor. In 1885 a new songbook, *Songs of Victory,* came from the *Gospel Trumpet* press then located in Williamston, Michigan. This was the first book ever published by the press. It contained ninety-four new songs, mostly composed by Warner and J. C. Fisher. This book "lyricized the theology and the spirit of the movement in such a way that it became even more joyful, inspiring, and contagious..." (J. Smith, 1980, 66). States the book's preface: "It is a fact well known ... that the hymns of the past fail to express the glorious Light and Liberty, Grace, Truth, and the Power the Free and Holy Church has attained in this blessed evening light. Hence the Lord has marvelously given us these NEW SONGS, that we may more fully sing the Joy and Victory we have in the Lord Jesus Christ."

Truth lies in restored relationships between a believer and God and among believers. It is expressed well in spirited song that focuses on Jesus Christ and exudes joy in the Spirit. It calls for wholeness of life and wholeness of the church, both by God's grace. Warner was on mission for such truth.

All People Welcome!

Included in the *Songs of Victory* collection were Warner's "I'm Redeemed," "I Ought to Love My Savior," and "The Evening Light." Witnesses this latter song:

> "Free from babel, in the Spirit,
> Free to worship God aright;
> Joy and gladness we're receiving,
> O how sweet this evening light!"

Joining this call to freedom and this sense of spontaneous joy was the conviction that all believers are equally a part of the church by the action of God. This dramatic stance attracted to the evolving movement socially oppressed people. Warner, for instance, refused to discriminate against African Americans who chose to attend his revival meetings. Many of them knew this and did come.

The "Floating Bethel" built by George Clayton and used on the
Ohio River for evangelistic services.
Used by D. S. and Frances Warner in the fall and winter of 1893.

In 1890 he was preaching in Mississippi. Blacks joined the crowd each night. Soon a mob of about seventy-five angry and armed white people appeared. A brick came flying through a window and Warner's face was bloodied. He was rescued and recovered in a nearby secluded cabin with the help of local friends. With safety and time to reflect there, he composed the words to the hymn "Who Will Suffer with the Savior?"

It was clear that a stance insisting that racial as well as denominational barriers have no place in the church would be painful and very dangerous, but the truth is the truth. The church is God's, not the domain of only white folks or of whoever controls the power within churchly institutions! Today an unusually high percentage of African American believers are part of the Church of God movement.

Their presence has (1) heightened the focus on Christian experience as opposed to sterile theological abstractions, (2) nurtured a musical tradition that encourages self-expression in worship and the narrative (testimnony) sharing of pivotal life experiences, (3) forced a multi-cultural caution about premature rigidities in truth formulations or institutional structures, and (4) pointed to the necessity of social as well as individual implications of being a Christian. At least in part, this has been enabled by the early attitudes and courageous actions of Daniel Warner.

These liberating attitudes and actions also extended to the issue of the leadership role of women in the church. In Warner's time it was not legal for women to vote in public elections. Many Christians excluded them from all teaching and preaching roles, claiming biblical support for such discrimination. But in God's church, Warner judged, there no longer is male or female. The church belongs to God, not to human leaders of any gender![16] In fact:

> There was never a time in the history of the [Church of God] movement, in fact, when women were not considered an essential part of the leadership. It was a striking aspect of the early days to see women functioning on the same level as men. Forty years before the time of woman's suffrage on a national level a great company of women were preaching, singing, writing and helping to determine the policies in this religious reform movement (J. Smith, 1955, 125).

In God's church, all people are welcome.

Transitions Good and Bad

In early 1887 another moral crisis rose to trouble Warner's ministry. J. C. Fisher, Warner's publishing partner since the *Trumpet*'s early days, decided he had a right to divorce his wife Allie. Assuming that this was being driven by the fact that Fisher had fallen in love with a younger woman, Warner insisted that he repent or leave the publishing work. Fisher did not repent, did divorce and remarry, and left the *Trumpet*.

The resulting financial and leadership crisis was addressed quickly to spare the movement any unnecessary public disgrace and to stabilize the operation during the unwelcome transition. The arrival of Enoch Byrum on the grounds of the camp meeting in Bangor, Michigan, provided the answer. Enoch was that older brother of Noah who had been so impressed with Warner in the earlier revival in Prospect, Indiana. He had no printing or managerial experience, except having been a farmer. But he had the necessary Christian commitment and literary skill—he was a student at Otterbein University. He also had the needed $900 to buy out Fisher.

Byrum immediately became publisher and business manager of the little company and would replace Warner as editor on Warner's death in 1895. These two men were very different, but graciously complementary. Byrum was not the electric public speaker. He was an executive who could put a ministry on firm business ground. Warner was the inspirer who communicated the vision that launched the ministry. He was an "artist in things of the spirit," a man who generated "undying loyalty in all who knew him and loved him" (Brown, 1951, 132–33). So now it was Warner and Byrum who were left to carry on.

With this leadership and financial crisis solved, another new songbook was published, *Anthems from the Throne* (148 songs, 90 set to music, edited by Warner and B. E. Warren). Warner's busy preaching schedule forced a slow shifting of the editorial work to Enoch Byrum, who kept Warner supplied with quantities of the *Gospel Trumpet* and the books being published. Warner would sell them on the road to help finance his traveling ministry. Three months after his first wife Sarah died in May 1893, in Cincinnati of typhoid fever and peritonitis, he married Frankie Miller, a member of his evangelistic company. Together with others, they carried on an influential evangelistic ministry for the short time that Daniel had left.

Shortly after the wedding the Warners were in Pittsburgh, Pennsylvania, to board the crew of the "Floating Bethel." This was a sunken barge that G. T. Clayton had bought, refloated, and prepared as a gospel tabernacle on the water. The idea was to travel on the Ohio and Mississippi Rivers, living on board and tying up at towns along the way to hold meetings and establish new congregations of believers. Daniel and Frankie spent the fall and winter of 1893 on the water and in a series of river towns, mixing experimentation and evangelism, all for the glory of God. By May 1894, they were back in

Grand Junction supervising the volunteer labor that was erecting for them a little two-story home on a piece of land parceled out from the campgrounds.[17] It was here that in little more than one year Daniel Warner would spend his last days.

Questions for Group Discussion

1. Prophetic voices that call people to "come out" often judge harshly and therefore are judged harshly. How do Christians remain true to their convictions and, at the same time, build and not burn bridges linking sisters and brothers in Christ?

2. Marriages today are often under siege. This is true of highly committed and very visible, even vulnerable Christian leaders. Is there anything to be learned from reviewing the tragic departure of Sarah Warner?

3. Daniel Warner had a strong anti-organization bias that has influenced much of the history of the Church of God movement. Do you agree with Herbert Riggle's judgment that this bias was a basic weakness of the movement's pioneers? How can the work of the church be carried on effectively without violating the integrity of the church itself?

4. Warner was relentlessly valiant for the truth, in part because of a sense of urgency. He believed that time was short. Christ soon would return. Has the church today lost this sense of urgency? How should the expected return of Christ be related to our Christian lives?

5. What exactly is "truth" for Christians? Is it a set of creedal statements to which all must agree? How can believers be convictional without being closed to the emergence of a fuller understanding of truth at each stage of spiritual and intellectual development?

Notes

1. See Phillips 1979, chapter one. After Warner's death the operation would move to Moundsville, West Virginia, in 1898, and in 1906 to Anderson, Indiana, its longterm and current location.

2. A Morrison family helped host this meeting. See John A. Morrison, *As the River Flows* (1962), chapter 5.

3, See Warner's report of the St. James meeting in the *Gospel Trumpet,* August 15, 1887.

4. Currently found as "I Ought to Love My Savior," in *Worship the Lord: Hymnal of the Church of God* (Warner Press, 1989), 461.

5. See Warner, *Gospel Trumpet*, July 15, 1884.

6. For the full text of the poem, see Appendix D.

7. Warner's sensitivity to scholarship is reflected in this little book. He speaks of having twelve different Bible translations before him as he writes (3). Elsewhere he refers to "the Vatican Manuscript, which is chiefly the basis of our Greek text" (9).

8. In 1870 the Kalamazoo and South Haven Railroad arrived in Grand Junction, running east and west to connect Kalamazoo with a good harbor on Lake Michigan, in part for the transport of local timber. In the next year the Chicago and Michigan Lake Shore Railroad came, running north and south. See *History of Berrien and VanBuren Counties, Michigan,* 432.

9. There was no local congregation or church building in Grand Junction associated with these "saints," as they became known locally. So they worshiped in homes of the area as families made them available. One family was Joseph and Mary Smith, parents of "Freddie" Smith, only six years old when the saints first arrived and later to become a prominent leader in this movement. See J. Smith, 1955, 104–105.

10. See the biography of Barney Warren by Axchie Bolitho, *To the Chief Singer* (1942), chapter 2. For the auto-

biography of the colorful "Mother" Sarah Smith, see *Familiar Names and Faces* (Moundsville, W. Va: Gospel Trumpet Co., 1902), 182–248. Warner later would marry Frances Miller.

11. *A Brief History of the Church of God in Alabama* (White): 1891-1966, 3.

12. Noah Byrum, "Early Days of Our Publishing Work," *Gospel Trumpet,* March 8, 1941.

13. Note the section "Truth: More Pursued Than Captured" (Strege, 1991, 53–57) featuring the important accomplishment of Dr. Otto F. Linn (1887–1965) in refining Warner's position in a more sophisticated and open manner.

14. See Merle Strege, "Seeing Eye To Eye: D. S. Warner's Approach to Conflict," *Vital Christianity,* January, 1990, 16–17. Warner is said to have "used the power of the editor's office to eliminate contrary opinion."

15. Warner, *Gospel Trumpet*, December 14, 1893, 1.

16. See Juanita Evans Leonard, ed., *Called to Minister, Empowered to Serve: Women in Ministry* (1989). This book was written on the occasion of the first national consultation on women in ministry and missions of the Church of God movement and contains the writings of eleven prominent women currently providing leadership to the movement.

17. This home was restored to like-new condition as part of the 1992 centennial celebration of Warner Camp. Somewhat like Warner's "flying ministry," the home is still available for guests who come from busy schedules to remember, rest, and reflect on their own Christian service.

8

Conceiving a Movement
(1886–1895)

A vigorous reform movement clearly was now underway. Enoch Byrum was overseeing considerable progress in the publishing work at Grand Junction, Michigan. By 1891 there was a home owned there for the workers, new equipment in operation, and the circulation of the *Gospel Trumpet* had risen to eight thousand. A German edition of the *Trumpet* now was available and there was a children's paper, the *Shining Light*.

While staunchly opposed to denominational distinctives as a means of self-definition, this movement, now growing rapidly, needed some sense of corporate identity. It was more than the one man, Daniel Warner. It surely was not intended to be just another human institution. It was believed to be a move of God! But how should such a marvelous thing be understood in relation to the flow of biblical history and the rest of the Christian community?

Foretold by the Prophets

Any group self-understanding would have to be biblical and non-denominational to fit the theological vision of Daniel Warner. Warner again was the primary person to rise to the occasion and begin to articulate such a group self-understanding. He sensed that his physical strength was waning and that his traveling days were limited. He was having attacks of rheumatism and severe coughing spells more frequently. So he applied to the Army for a disability pension to help with medical expenses.[1] More importantly, he knew that a movement of God was gaining momentum in response to his ministry and those of his colleagues and that he yet had an opportunity, even a responsibility, to help shape its character and future.

One way that he approached this task was by inventing a special jargon, a provocative vocabulary that "produces an adhesive effect, holding the members of the group close to each other" (Clear 1977, 40). "Sectism" was designated a prime enemy of the church. "Babylon" was now the commonly used biblical metaphor for the church's wilderness captivity by all things human. "Come-Outers" were said to be enlightened believers who step out on faith and break free of Babylon. As early as March 26, 1878, shortly after his expulsion from the West Ohio Eldership, Warner refers in his journal to people in sects as "Babylon's children," with Babylon including "about all Protestant churchism." These and other judgmental terms joined to give shape and voice to "a powerful mythos" (Strege 1993, 10), especially when they were perceived to have biblical roots in a particular way of interpreting the message of the Bible's apocalyptic literature.

In Warner's earliest extensive treatment of his own views on the holiness reform and its relation to sectarianism (*Bible Proofs of the Second Work of Grace,* 1880), he saw clear biblical roots. The key verses were Hebrews 12:25–29, which he saw as the Old Testament's prophetic description of the "great work of holiness" in his own time (Dieter 249). Warner applied the warnings of Ezekiel to the leaders of sectarian churches:

> I will seek out my sheep and will deliver them out of all places [sectarian coops] where they have been scattered [into several hundred parties] in the cloudy and dark day.... The perfect reign of the Messiah ... is to succeed the dark days of party confusion (1880, 376).

Such visionary interpretations had dramatic contemporary relevance—and were preached with great force! A significant development then emerged in the self-understanding of key leaders of the young Church of God movement around the time that the publishing work moved to Grand Junction, Michigan, in 1886. Partly, it was the obvious maturing of a ministry in the midst of a strengthening sense of "family" among the dedicated Trumpet workers. In the 1886 move the work "was ready to leave the cradle for good. The family and the paper had become the center, the living embryo, of what was now a movement" (Hetrick 14).

But there was more. It was the acquiring of a new way of establishing the movement's evolving self-understanding, a way now being drawn increasingly from biblical prophecy. Seventh-day Adventism was strong in this part of Michigan and soon Warner was well acquainted with the work of a leading Adventist editor and writer, Uriah Smith (see Schwarz 81, 185, 192). Smith had developed a complex interpretive system that coordinated a reading of biblical prophecy with the emergence and historical role of Adventism (U. Smith 1882). To this system Warner initially was repelled, then was attracted—with refinements.

Warner, a skilled debater, studied Smith's writing with care[2] and came to oppose his application of these biblical texts to Adventism. The basic disagreement between Smith and Warner involves the identity of the lamblike beast of Revelation 13:11–19. Earliest Adventism had associated it with the Saturday Sabbath. Smith saw it symbolizing the United States of America, while Warner now believed that it symbolized Protestantism (Stanley 1990, 78). Warner was especially concerned that Adventist theology applied the "cleansing of the sanctuary" concept to a cleansing in heaven to begin in 1844 (Warner 1903, 38). He saw the cleansing related instead to the holiness reform of his own day. For persons in Indiana, Ohio, and Michigan who were intrigued at the time by such eschatological issues, Adventists and Church of God pioneers clearly became competitors on the interpretive scene. There was agreement, however, that these biblical

The Lord Our Shepherd

"When he has brought out all his own, he goes on ahead of them, and his sheep follow him because they know his voice."—John 10:4

Daniel S. Warner

THE LORD OUR SHEPHERD
Uriah E. Hallman

1 We'll fol - low the Lord all the way, (all the way,)
2 The sheep of His pas - ture are one, (all are one,)
3 There's joy in the fold of the Lord, (of the Lord,)
4 By riv - ers of peace we are led, (we are led,)

1 And close to our Shep - herd we'll stay; How bless - ed to know,
2 Yea, one as the Fa - ther and Son; They're all of one mind,
3 We walk in the light of His Word; We love to o - bey
4 In pas - tures of love we are fed; We ev - er re - joice

1 as we jour - ney be - low, He's with us by night and by day!
2 as their Shep - herd de-signed, They fol - low and serve Him a - lone.
3 all the Sav - ior doth say, Thus liv - ing in ho - ly ac - cord.
4 at the sound of His voice, Re - deemed by the blood He has shed.

We will fol - low, ev - er fol - low In the
We will fol - low on, fol - low on In

134

foot - steps   of the Sav - ior;   We will fol - low,
Je - sus' steps, the   Sav - ior's steps;   Fol - low   on,

ev - er fol - low   In His path - way bright and clear.
we'll   fol - low   on

materials portray a map of the church's history from the first to the second coming of Christ.

Warner became absorbed in Uriah Smith's general system of interpretation.[3] Soon, having altered a few key details, Warner was himself presenting this general plan of presumed biblical prophecy, now as a prophetic framework and a dramatic rationale for the young Church of God movement! This plan began appearing with the October 15, 1883, issue of the *Gospel Trumpet* when Warner identified the first "beast" of Revelation 13 as Roman Catholicism and the second as the Protestant "churches" that sprang from it. The one was a harlot, the other the harlot's daughters.

Shortly Warner would be working on a major manuscript, *The Cleansing of the Sanctuary* (1903), that would have to be completed after his death by his friend Herbert Riggle. A *Gospel Trumpet* article by this title appeared under Warner's name in the June 1, 1887, issue. This was the first time he developed from biblical prophecy a chronological timetable for the reformation of the church. Now being seen was "an exact parallel" between the description in Nehemiah 2–6 and "the present work of cleansing the sanctuary, or restoring the complete walls of salvation." In the April 7, 1892, *Trumpet* is a large chart detailing the key dates of church history with their prophetic references, all culminating in the "fall of sectism, A. D. 1880." That was the general time of Warner's "new commission" and bold steps beyond the bounds of standard sectism.

A key verse was Zechariah 14:7 which says that "it shall come to pass that at evening time it shall be light." Was it not now the "evening time," with God's full and final light coming fast to those who would receive? Were not the walls of salvation being restored fully? Martin Luther had recovered justification by faith from Roman darkness (sixteenth century). John Wesley had reintroduced true Christian holiness (eighteenth century). Now Warner and his colleagues were catching it all up and bringing it to maturity by seeing the final gathering into one of all the saved and sanctified saints of God. This vision was exhilarating and, as usual, was caught up in lyrics written by Warner and still sung in the movement of the Church of God:

> Brighter days are sweetly dawning,
>> O the glory looms in sight!
> For the cloudy day is waning,
>> And the evening shall be light.

> Lo! the ransomed are returning,
>> Robed in shining crystal white;
> Leaping, shouting home to Zion,
>> Happy in the evening light.

It may be that there was "a moment, heavy with destiny, when Warner felt in his heart that God, in the year 1880, was breaking again into history, that it was foretold by the prophets, and that Warner was a central figure, being used of God to usher in the last phase of history before the end of the age" (Reardon 22). The scattered "saints," the courageous come-outers, were no longer an isolated and insignificant phenomenon. They had the role of heralding the initiation of

God's ultimate will for the church. They represented the leading edge of the "last reformation."

Convictions long held about church divisions and heart holiness now were combined by Daniel Warner, under apparent biblical direction, to create a sense of destiny. This focusing of identity greatly accelerated a "movement" consciousness. While not date setters and not expecting an earthly millennium, Warner came to see the work of restoring the pure and united church as a sign of the rapidly approaching return of Christ. There was the urgency of a God-ordained mission in the "last days," an urgency generating a self-conscious "movement" now being driven by a biblical vision. The themes of unity, holiness, and biblical prophecy blended and were conveyed powerfully by the preaching skill of Daniel Warner.

In Warner's early ministry, the primary theme (beyond salvation itself) was Christian unity. Then it was holiness and unity, and finally it became unity and holiness in light of bibilcal prophecy. Warner thus was involved in "two different interpretations of the movement's reason for being" (Strege 1993, 12). One is represented well by his song "The Bond of Perfectness" that highlights the unity of Christians enabled by the sanctifying power of God. Here is a classic expression of the clear relationship seen by Warner between the sanctifying experience (perfectness) and the intended unity of God's people. The chorus states:

> Beloved how this perfect love,
>   Unites us all in Jesus!
> One heart, and soul, and mind we prove,
>   The union heaven gave us.

The other interpretation of the movement's reason for being, seen in Warner's later writings, is represented well by the work of William Schell. In 1893 Schell published *Biblical Trace of the Church,* the first major work to define the movement's evolving identity by a church-historical interpretation of the Bible's prophetic material.[4] There also is Schell's song "Biblical Trace of the Church."[5] Here the movement's identity

The "Gospel Van" built by J. H. Rupert and used in England in the 1890s. Pictured here in 1894 are Lena Shoffner, Hattie Rupert, and J. H. Rupert (who soon went on to Germany).

is pictured as a prophetically foretold instrument of God. In the last days it was to help regather from divided Romanism and Protestantism the one church comprised of all God's children.

This view became widely influential in the Church of God movement for decades, largely through the ministry of the third editor of the *Gospel Trumpet,* F. G. Smith.[6] It finally began to be questioned widely, especially during and after the 1940s.[7]

Both of these approaches to the movement's self-understanding are deeply resident in at least one phase of the life and thought of Warner. Herbert Riggle recalls attending his first camp meeting in Perryville, Pennsylvania, in August 1893. Warner did most of the preaching, all doctrinal. Riggle reports:

> The great fundamental truths of full salvation and holiness, the church of God, Bible unity, the downfall of sect-Babylon and the command to come out of her, the great

apostasy, the last reformation, divine healing, etc., were set forth with boldness and authority. On the last Sunday of the meeting, in the morning service, when the hour of preaching arrived, Brother Warner leaped into the pulpit and cried, "Fire, fire, FIRE." He then read 2 Thess. 2:3–8, and emphasized the words "whom the Lord shall consume with the spirit of his mouth, and shall destroy with the brightness of his coming." His subject was "The Consuming and Destroying of Apostate Christianity"— the consuming fulfilled in the present reform work, and accomplished "with the spirit of his mouth" (the flaming truth accompanied by the fire of holiness)....

For three and one half hours the message came forth like mighty thunder-peals. People sat spell-bound during all that time. I trembled under the mighty power of God. Under such preaching, it was not difficult to find the highway that leads to Zion. And the ransomed of the Lord came home with everlasting joy (1924, 59–60).

Such vision and powerful preaching had done much to generate a significantly new movement among God's people. The movement, universal in intent, soon was having a trans-denominational and multicultural impact. Geography was no barrier. The lack of air travel could not ground these "flying ministers."

After the Battle

In 1882 the *Gospel Trumpet* was being read in Canada. Warner and his evangelistic company followed up by holding a series of meetings in Ontario in 1888. Warner spent two and a half months in 1892 laboring in Southern California, after holding meetings in Missouri, Iowa, and Kansas on his way west.

A Benjamin Elliott in San Diego, California, felt called to evangelize Spanish-speaking people. If only he had the money to sail toward Mexico on God's special mission, he would be an enthusiastic missionary.

Tombstone, about 1896   Tombstone today

Elliott met Warner in Los Angeles. Warner, somehow knowing Elliott's call and need, pressed the money in his hand! In that moment cross-cultural mission was born in the Church of God movement.[8]

The first camp meeting on the sixty acre tract of land along Lake Lester just north of Grand Junction, Michigan, (June 1892) saw 145 new believers baptized in the lake, with some thirty ministers present from twelve states and Canada (Confer 28). By 1893 workers from America were pulling a "gospel van" around England, Ireland, and Scotland. It was loaded with papers and books from the Gospel Trumpet Company back in Michigan.

One of these workers was J. H. Rupert. In 1894 he moved from England to Hamburg, Germany, to locate friends and relatives of the "saints" in the United States. He was able to distribute a German edition of the *Gospel Trumpet* now being published in America.

Warner and those inspired by him were experimenting, risking, always reaching out. They made no distinction between church and mission. To be in the church was to be on mission.

To be in the church was not to belong to some denomination, culture, race, gender, or nation. It's God's church! All who believe belong.

In 1895 there were at least twenty-five annual grove meetings, fourteen camp meetings, and several general assemblies carrying the banner and burden of the Church of God movement. Because Warner wrote most of the early literature and songs and typically spoke at key gatherings his works became recognized as standard. There also was an active children's school on the Grand Junction, Michigan, campgrounds, something that Warner had worked to have initiated.[9] Warner was planning a broadened curriculum for the continuing education of the gospel workers, to include courses in history, music, and Bible.

Warner was preaching for the present, while writing and hoping to educate for the future. He also was planning a world tour, although poor health prevented his ever going. The movement was spreading through the printed word and other workers, even if Warner could not always continue his exhausting travel schedule.

Also in 1895 G. W. Bailey and J. C. Peterman, movement ministers, arrived in Grand Forks, North Dakota, where some people interested in holiness were holding cottage meetings. Soon there was a congregation of the Church of God in that place. Also, having seen an advertisement about books from the Gospel Trumpet Company in the United States, John Alla-ud-Din Khan of India sent for all he could get, was moved by the message, and immediately subscribed to the *Gospel Trumpet* (Royster 73–78).

The movement now had crossed oceans and cultures. Soon it would proceed on, but without the leadership of Daniel Warner. Little strength was left in his frail body. After the Grand Junction campmeeting in the summer of 1895, Warner wrote one of his last poems. Calling it "After the Battle," he seemed to sense that his own life was nearing its end and that God's work on earth soon would be complete.

The poem's themes of hope, joy, and liberty are those of

Warner's whole ministry. The final stanza reads:

> Amen! amen! let heaven shout,
>   And earth break forth in song!
>   A thousand camps, ten thousand groves,
>   In every city throng.
>   Along the rivers, o'er the sea,
>   In Jesus' mighty name,
>   The present truth that set us free,
>   To all aloud proclaim.

Death came on December 12, 1895, at his new home on the edge of the campgrounds in Grand Junction, Michigan. The immediate cause was pneumonia. Warner was only fifty-three.

The funeral service was conducted on the fifteenth at the Grand Junction campground by William G. Schell. In the *Gospel Trumpet* issue of December 19 he reported to grieving saints far and wide. After the funeral sermon was over, Schell wrote, "the remains were exhibited to a large weeping audience."

The body was then taken to the little cemetery just west of the campground where it was laid to rest.[10] "Before leaving the grave we vowed eternal submission to the will of God." The obituary that appeared in the same issue was written by Warner's successor in the editorship, E. E. Byrum. Said Byrum:

> The life of our dear brother was one wholly devoted to God. He was not slow to rebuke sin, and was ever ready to defend the truth, fearing not the face of man.... His pen was as a pen of a ready writer, and also being fluent in speech and endowed with many God-given gifts and a deep understanding of the Scriptures, was thereby enabled to do much effective work for the Master, and give spiritual food to multitudes of starving souls.

Warner had been a man driven by a vision centered in Christian holiness and unity. He was convinced that "Brighter days are sweetly dawning /O the glory looms in sight! /For the cloudy day is waning, /And the ev'ning shall be light." According to historian Charles Brown, Warner, having finally found an integrated vision of Christian holiness and unity (during the formative period 1877–1881), "spent the rest of his life trying to find ways, means, and methods of making that illumination fruitful in the restoration of the church both ideally and practically" (1954, 110–11). He was a "liberationist" leader. "In an era of unrest and rebellion against 'formalism' in the established churches," observes Aubrey Forrest, "he offered a dynamic leadership. He thundered against the sins of his day like an ancient prophet" (54).

Daniel Warner was a "movement" man. He was a pioneer, not a settler. He had the feeling of being swept along by something that was initiated from above. He possessed little of the prestige or goods of this world. Rather, his significance emerges from what possessed him. God had spoken. God was acting to sanctify and unify the church. This belief grasped Warner and to it he gave his life. God, Warner believed, wants no artificial divisions among his people. Therefore, Warner envisioned no narrow sectarian band of followers but challenged believers to follow truth wherever it leads and to reach their hands in fellowship to all people whose hearts have been renewed in Christ. The lyrics of one of the many hymns he composed combines these themes, emphasizing repeatedly in the chorus, "we will follow, ever follow, in His [Jesus'] pathway bright and clear" (see the hymn, "The Lord Our Shepherd").

Andrew Byers, one of Warner's many "sons and daughters" in the ministry, once stood by the grave of Warner. It is a quiet setting on the grounds of what now is called Warner Camp about one mile north of the little town of Grand Junction, Michigan. "Here nature undisturbed, through the succession of bursting buds of spring, refreshing dews of summer, sighing breezes and gently falling leaves of autumn, and rigorous storms of winter covering all with a shroud of snow, is heard to speak silently but eloquently of the brief cycle of life on this earth." In this profound speaking, Byers remembered his mentor and friend, Daniel Warner. He reflected on "the wonderful accomplishment crowded into that short career." Then Byers felt faced with a choice. "Come what may of toil and self-sacrifice in the Christian service, come what may of reproach and persecution for Christ's sake, 'let me die the death of the righteous, and let my last end be like his' " (Byers 1921, 477).

A century now has passed since Warner's death. The physical surroundings of his grave still symbolize what his ministry was all about. His remains lie in that simple grove of trees, secluded from much of the world. He never sought popularity for himself and never has captured the spotlight of the larger Christian community. His name, memory, and vision, however, live on, especially within the Church of God movement.

Within yards of his resting place today is a missionary lodge, cabins for youth camps, and a tabernacle and bookstore for proclaiming and spreading God's Word. Mission, Christian nurture, and gospel publication, these were the burdens of Daniel Warner. He was God's man, committed to wholeness of life by sanctifying grace and oneness in the church by the same grace. It's God's church and we are to be God's people.

One more geographic note. Only about one hundred yards from Warner's simple grave are the same railroad tracks that often carried him on long evangelistic tours, accompanied by tons of Christian literature, much of which he wrote or edited. Standing today by his resting place, one soon will hear a train approaching, out of sight only because of a stretch of trees and underbrush. It is as if the memory of Warner's passion for the gospel of Jesus Christ were yet calling for all of us to leave our places of origin and comfort, our fears of rejection and death, and launch out for Christ!

In a significant way, Warner's early death paralleled that of Moses. Moses was able to see the land of promise, but it was not his to see the promise fulfilled for all the people. The land Warner saw was a place of real obedience to God, where lives are transformed and sanctified, where the church sheds its many destructive divisions and becomes one as God's people on mission in this world. Since this is God's will, a divine promise, something of Warner's vision should live in the hearts and lives of God's people today. The promise is on its way to fulfillment in God's way, at God's timing. It is for us to see the vision, believe the promise, be faithful, and journey on.

Beyond the Fire

In 1896, soon after his death, Warner's last book appeared, *Salvation, Present, Perfect, Now or Never.* Despite Warner's poor health and extremely busy schedule, between 1881 and 1895 the Gospel Trumpet Company had grown "from a tiny, almost one-man operation to a reasonably well-established business whose impact was even then reaching far around the world. Periodicals, songbooks, books, tracts, and booklets were pouring from its presses and would continue despite the death of its founder" (Phillips 1979, 47). In 1895 about 7,500 copies of the *Gospel Trumpet* were being published weekly.

This publishing was being done out of the following statement of vision that then appeared regularly on the masthead of the *Gospel Trumpet:* "DEFINITE, RADICAL, and ANTI-SECTARIAN, sent forth in the name of the Lord Jesus Christ, for the publication of full Salvation, Divine Healing of the Body, and the Unity of all true Christians in 'the faith once delivered to the saints.' " It has been observed that "it was not accidental that the usual term, 'nonsectarian,' was not used. The movement was consciously and vigorously anti. Not only was it anti-sectarian, but anti almost anything that was interpreted as characterisitc of any denominational group. In general, it was held, the denominational world exists to justify evil under the guise of good" (Clear 1977, 41–42).

The last issue of the *Trumpet* to be published at Grand Junction, Michigan, would be June 30, 1898. The following issue originated from Moundsville, West Virginia, where the press moved and would prosper until its permanent move in 1906 to Anderson, Indiana. The mood remained very Warner-like, evangelistic and expansionist. Warner's successor in the editorship, Enoch Byrum, sent this message to all *Gospel Trumpet* subscribers on January 5, 1899:

We are by faith moving out upon the promises of God and arranging to increase the spread of the pure gospel to every nation and land, and ask the united prayers and cooperation of the brethren and all those interested in the welfare of perishing souls.

God's guiding and protecting hand seemed to be on this work. Harold Phillips calls his writing of the history of this publishing ministry a "miracle of survival" (1979). One dramatic event seems to summarize so many others. The night after the trainload of machinery and the Trumpet Family pulled out of Grand Junction in its relocation to West Virginia, the vacated publishing property and the buildings that had housed the workers mysteriously burned to the ground! There were no injuries, no insurance, no sure explanation,[11] but escape from near tragedy into an enlarging future.

Probably the fire started by sparks from a passing train, with few people now around to notice quickly and put it out in time. It was a night of historic irony. The little village of Grand Junction for twelve years had hosted a small community of Christians with a burning passion for the good news of Christ. From that little railroad crossing they had fanned the flames of a movement far and wide. Now they had moved on and the place was in ashes. Somehow it symbolized a key part of their message to the church. Structures are fragile and passing. So are pioneers like Daniel Warner. But much of what he dreamed, sang, preached, and wrote would form a living legacy with a definite future. A comment Warner once made about himself puts him in proper perspective. J. W. Byers recalled a time when he asked Warner to preach in his place, otherwise Byers would have to preach with Warner present. Byers confessed, "Brother Warner, I simply could not preach in the presence of such a great man as you are." Warner was moved by the compliment. He then put his arms around Byers and said gently, "God bless you, my brother. I am only one of God's little ones." Warner was right; he was little, except for the grace of God. As the hymn lyric puts it, "little is much when God is in it!" God had been in the life of Daniel Warner.

Questions for Group Discussion

1. Daniel Warner and his associates never claimed to build a church, another denomination. To the contrary, they claimed merely to have "discerned the Lord's body" and thus had decided to abide in it alone. Is this possible? Must Christians function within given church organizations, thus automatically building rival "churches"?

2. The early call to "come out" of denominationalism, at its best, meant to come with us to participation in God's true, only, and humanly unencumbered church. But how easily "come with us" deteriorates into or at least is heard to mean "come to us," for we finally and fully have come into possession of the truth. How does the Church of God movement itself avoid being sectarian?

3. Warner's song "The Bond of Perfectness," includes the vision of Christians being united into "one heart and soul and mind." Does oneness of mind suggest a singleness of thinking, a unity based on common beliefs? Doctrinally and organizationally, what does it take to be really united as Christians?

4. Developed late in Warner's ministry was reliance on a special interpretation of the biblical books of Daniel and Revelation as a way of understanding the role of the Church of God movement in God's plan. How appropriate, even necessary is reliance on such interpretation today?

5. Tolerance is an admired virtue in our culture. Often we now watch in silence what Warner would have denounced aggressively. How much of this change is a reflection of a proper flexibility that we have achieved in a multi-cultural world, and how much is merely our moral decay and complacence?

6. Are we prepared to relinquish our human loyalties and church traditions to be "soft clay in the Spirit's hands"?

7. Our world today is so "tribe" conscious. We are good at discriminating and persecuting those who are not "one of us." In the church, how can you work toward making real the belief that all who believe belong?

Notes

1. In 1890, when applying for a veteran's disability pension, Warner described his problem as "lung trouble, and bronchial, a chronic cough, which has been by some physicians called consumption. I have not been able ever since the war to do half a man's work at manual labor." He received a pension of $12 per month until his death.

2. Daniel Warner's personal copy of Uriah Smith's 1882 book (hardback, more than 800 pages long) now is in the archives of Anderson University. It includes handwritten marginal notes by Warner, clear evidence of his extensive interaction with this material.

3. Dieter reports, n. 40, 282: "In their efforts to develop a rationale for their movements and their place within the Christian Church, Warner and the other radicals under discussion exhibited a classic illustration of a persistent Christian tradition which may be traced back to Joachim of Fiore (ca. 1145–1202). Joachim, out of his study of the Scriptures and in his earnestness for reform of the church as he knew it, divided the history of the church into seven periods, dominant among which were the Constantinian fall and restitution of the church under a new Constantine in the end time. His further division of history into the dispensations of the Father, Son, and Spirit, with the "age of the Spirit" as the greatest and last, is especially represented in its long passage through men and movements in subsequent church history. It recurs in the concept of the 'Holy Ghost and last Dispensation' which ... was so important to the holiness movement and particularly to the perfectionsim of the radical reformers. They saw their age as corresponding with the end time, which Joachim, in his scheme, had seen as the time 'when the Spirit and Life' would be in the church in 'the time of the eternal Gospel.' "

4. For perspective, see John Stanley, "Unity and Diversity: Interpreting the Book of Revelation in the Church of God (Anderson)," *Wesleyan Theological Journal* 25:2 (fall 1990).

5. Appearing as song twenty in *Songs of the Evening*

Light (Gospel Trumpet, 1897), it traces church history by successive references to "the church of the morning bright," "the sun went down," "the sun coming up next day," and "we welcome the evening light." Reading church history through a particular scheme of prophetic interpretation, Schell speaks of the "long dreary Papal night! Twelve hundred and sixty years," and then moves to the "cloudy day—Three hundred and fifty years" [Protestantism].

The preface to this songbook begins with these words: "We are in the evening of the last dispensation of time. In fulfillment of the prophecy "at evening time it shall be light" (Zech. 14:7), the pure gospel is shining now as it never has shone since the days of primitive Christianity. The ransomed of the Lord are returning from their apostatized condition." Here is a clear expression of one view of the movement's reason for being.

6. F. G. Smith was converted at age ten in a children's meeting at the Bangor, Michigan, campgrounds. His parents had hosted many of the earliest meetings of the "saints" in that area. When the Trumpet family left Grand Junction for West Virginia in 1898, Smith moved with them as a young member.

7. See Barry Callen (1969), chapter four, where "the disparagement of prophetic enthusiasms" is identified as one of the central pivots of change in the movement's history.

8. See Maurice Caldwell, in *Church of God Missions* (June, 1992), 2–3.

9. Sebastian Michels of South Haven, Michigan, provided key leadership initially. See Confer 30–32.

10. In 1927 Daniel's wife Frances (Miller) died and was buried here alongside him.

11. Likely the fire was started by sparks thrown from a passing train. See Noah Byrum, "Memories of Bygone Days," *Young People's Friend,* August 28, 1932, 3.

Daniel S. Warner's Name Remembered

The following are some of the more prominent ministries of the Church of God movement that have chosen to be identified by the name of Daniel Warner.

Warner Press,
Anderson, Indiana   1881 to present
Originally known as the Gospel Trumpet Company, the first organized ministry of the Church of God movement and currently the publishing house of the movement.

Warner Memorial Camp Meeting   1892 to present
Convenes annually in Grand Junction, Michigan, and is the site of the final home and death of Daniel Warner.

Warner Memorial University,
Eastland, Texas   1929–1933
A vigorous venture into higher education thatfell victim to the Great Depression.

Warner Pacific College,
Portland, Oregon   1937 to present
Known as Pacific Bible College until 1959, now a liberal arts institution.

Warner Auditorium   Built in 1961
Home of the mass meetings of the International Convention of the Church of God that convenes annually in Anderson, Indiana.

Warner Southern College,
Lake Wales, Florida   1968 to present
A liberal arts institution of higher ecucation established to serve primarily students in the southeastern United States.

A Lingering Legacy

We began by saying that stories shape us. Now we have retold the dramatic story of the life and ministry of Daniel Warner. The question that remains is, what does this story mean for us today? Should it shape our current attitudes and actions as we seek to be God's people? If so, how? Warner faced the final years of the nineteenth century. We face the end of the twentieth, in many ways a very different world.

The situation is symbolized well by a day in the fall of 1895, not long before Warner's death. The Gospel Trumpet Company was growing and needed to expand its limited facilities in Grand Junction, Michigan. A decision was made to add on to the building with help from some of the church men in the area. The diary of Noah Byrum describes this event:

It was decided to get a car load of sand, for plastering, from Lake Michigan beach at South Haven [ten miles west of Grand Junction]. A number of us took the team and drove to South Haven. Bro. D. S. Warner was one of the group. It took most of the day to haul the sand to the car. Brother Warner was not strong enough to do very much heavy manual labor. He thoroughly enjoyed the day and was vitally interested in the progress of the new building. He did not live to see it completed (1932, 3).[1]

A Lion Roaring

In 1920 Andrew Byers began publishing a series of sketch-es of the life and labors of Daniel Warner and several of his key associates (Feb 5, 1920). Byers spoke of these movement pioneers as having represented faithfully a "burning truth." These men and women were willing "to brave the necessary hardships in blazing the way for the establishment ... of the New Testament church in her undivided wholeness." Regarding this fresh path to Christian unity, historian Henry Wickersham speaks of Warner as "among the first in the nine-teenth century to preach full salvation outside of sectism" (1900, 301).

Judges another, Warner "was the boldest, most radical, most liberal thinker on Bible lines since the days of the apos-tles. At one sweep he stepped clear out into the very glory and simplicity of early Christianity and he pointed out the only way to church unity" (Berry, 1931, 9). Charles Naylor was more guarded. He knew Warner personally and "loved him with rev-erential affection." Nonetheless, Warner is said to have misin-terpreted many biblical texts in his single-minded enthusiasm for the cause that was his, especially in regard to prophetic biblical passages (1948, n.p.).

Warner was a lion roaring mightily against what he under-stood to be wrong in God's church. He was a poet, a dreamer, an idealist. He could be as relentless as he was gentle, always a despiser of evil and a passionate lover of truth. Obviously he had personal magnetism and unusual persuasive ability. People flocked to altars when he preached on holiness. They also "came out" of their denominations when he denounced the sects.

Warner was an evangelist. He had "a driving passion to proclaim the gospel and he drove himself relentlessly in that pursuit" (Hetrick 8). This ministry passion related to his mar-riages in positive and negative ways. He ended his first romance (Frances Stocking) because there was no commonali-ty of commitment to Christian ministry. When, in 1872, his first wife Tamzen died so young after giving birth to triplets, who also died, Warner filled the terrible void with intense ministry activity. He was both called by the Spirit of God and energized by the spirit of aching grief. Sarah, his second wife, separated from him in 1884. One reading of this tragic event is that "Warner sacrificed his second marriage on the altar of Truth. His wife could not abide his militant advocacy of the

The Gospel Trumpet Family, Grand Junction, 1885, in front of the Childrens' Home. Warner, seated in center with cane.

doctrine of the second blessing (or sanctification), and she left him" (Strege 1990, 17). The third wife, Frankie Miller, was a faithful and valuable ministry companion until Warner's death. His most intimate relationships were affected deeply by his call, vision, and relentless commitment to the evangelistic and reform cause.

The driving force of Warner's ministry, the power of his persuasiveness, was rooted in a spiritual vision. It also was nurtured by the pain of his own life experience. Robert Reardon reflects:

His Yoke Is Easy

"For my yoke is easy and my burden is light."—Matthew 11:30

Based on Matthew 11:28-30
Daniel S. Warner

HIS YOKE IS EASY
Barney E. Warren

1 I've found my Lord and He is mine, He won me by His love;
2 No oth-er Lord but Christ I know, I walk with Him a - lone;
3 He's dear-er to my heart than life, He found me lost in sin;
4 I've tried the road of sin, and found Its pros-pects all de - ceive;

1 I'll serve Him all my years of time And dwell with Him a - bove.
2 His streams of love for - ev - er flow With - in my heart, His throne.
3 He calmed the sea of in - ward strife And bade me come to Him.
4 I've proved the Lord, and joys a-bound, More than I could be - lieve.

His yoke is eas-y, His bur-den is light, I've found it so, I've found it so;

His serv - ice is my sweet-est de-light, His bless-ings ev - er flow.

I believe his anger and lashing out at the sects, his inveighing against organization of any kind within the church came from two sources. One was theological. He saw the church as a fellowship of born again and sanctified believers, something which can never be organized by people. The other source is emotional. It was the Eldership, a form of denominationalism, that had rejected him and set him aside. Out of this deep and lasting hurt came emotional power which drove the engine of his anger (21).

A leader's perspectives are not fully understood apart from knowing the story of that individual. Not even theological views are immune from the shaping influence of very human factors.[2]

A distinction should be drawn between reformer and prophet. When drawn, it helps to show the focus and the limits of Warner's ministry. The staggering magnitude of the task Warner undertook is characteristic of the prophet. Val Clear writes of this:

A reformer would have cut the problem up into smaller pieces and tackled them one at a time. But the prophet sees only the vision of the complete ideal which he seeks and he will accept no half-way measures. So Warner preached the elimination of the entire structure of organized Christianity. Since formal organization served as a harness holding in rein the Holy Spirit, it was a man-made obstacle to grace. It must go, and all God's children would then worship freely together in an undivided Zion. On several occasions Warner indicated that he expected to see this happen within a generation, perhaps within his own lifetime (1977, 41).

Formal church organizations did not disappear in Warner's lifetime and still have not a century later. Warner's prophetic voice, however, continues to speak. Responding to such a prophetic vision today requires practical reforming activity, not just the excitement of a grand vision. Andrew Byers notes

Warner's "pioneer position" from which he denounced "all things sectarian." Warner's work was "the initial, or birth stage of the reform." The task now moves to the "constructive" stage in which, rather than constantly denouncing the failures of the sects, the challenge is to manifest "those essential principles that characterize the church in her purity and entirety" (1921, 31–32). In other words, the rhetoric of criticism must shift to the rigor of implementation.

The task is to be God's church, not merely to criticize others for not being the church in its intended holiness and unity. See Appendix G for a contemporary statement of Warner's vision of the church and Appendix H for proposed guidelines by which Christians might interact across denominational lines for the good of the church's mission. There must be intentional movement from the abstract to the concrete.

The twentieth century has witnessed increased efforts on behalf of Christian unity (the "ecumenical" movement). The Church of God movement, however, has remained on the sidelines for the most part, pointing out false concepts of Christian unity. Warner seemed out ahead in his day. The Church of God movement has tended to lag behind in more recent times.

Respect Without Reverence

Herbert Riggle points out the crucial tension between the ideal and the practical. Reflecting back on the pioneer work of the Church of God movement in which Warner was so prominent, he observes:

> The early preaching of some of the first ministers was in some respects idealistic and theoretical to the exclusion of the practical. This is an honest confession of facts. It was easy to point out the sins and short-comings of the professed Christian world, and condemn these by the Word of God. It was not difficult for those who clearly discerned the body of Christ to hold before the people the ideal church of the New Testament from a purely

doctrinal standpoint.... Now, it is quite another thing to demonstrate in a practical way the ideal presented. We have found it many times more difficult. It is for this visible body of believers to present to the world a "glorious church, not having spot, or wrinkle, or any such thing; but that it should be holy and without blemish." This is the point. This is what the people expect of us. They have a right to (1924, 80).[3]

Warner, despite his strong anti-organizational bias, already had begun the process of experimenting with ways to make the ideal real without compromising the ideal. Andrew Byers concludes his study of the life and legacy of Warner with two important cautions and an attempt at identifying "essential principles" (1921, 24, 32–33). The first caution is that the Church of God movement must not itself act in a sectarian way. It would be sectarian, he says, if the movement ever yields to "any tendency to establish traditions, or to regard a past course as giving direction in all respects for the future, or to become self-centered and manifest a 'we are it' spirit and bar the door of progress against the entrance of further light and truth, or in any way to refuse fellowship with any others who may be Christians" (32). The prophetic ideal is to be maintained while ways are found to implement it in practical ways.

The second caution involves why we would study again the life and teachings of Warner. The reason should not be "exalting the man, but to illustrate what God can accomplish in and through one who is so devoted.... It is not assumed that Brother Warner was right on every point of doctrine or in every application of a Scriptural text" (33, 24).

He had his sidetracks and faulty judgments. For instance, Warner was interested in phrenology, the popular nineteenth-century "science" of reading human character traits by the shape of the head. He heard with appreciation a Dr. Everitt lecture on this in 1865. Occasionally Warner mentions this subject in his journal, mostly as a passing curiosity. During a stormy Sunday afternoon in May 1875, he passed the time with friends, reporting in his journal that he had "examined some heads."

More significantly, Charles Naylor's memory is that Warner expected all Christians to be brought into the Church of God movement in a single generation (1948, n. p.). If he really did think this, he was wrong. Clearly Warner was premature in stereotyping the restorationist and holiness movements of his time as just more of the problem. The holiness movement, for instance, was a hopeful even if limited sign of a trans-denominationalism in the power of the Spirit. In Warner's eyes, its failure was the reluctance to affirm his radical idealism that saw and insisted on more than others judged possible in this compromised world. His uncompromising idealism sometimes led to further division.

Was Warner guilty of excesses, premature judgments, faulty biblical interpretations? Yes, of course. But observe with Albert Gray that "in criticizing the excesses that existed among our early brethren we are doing just what they would do if they were still alive. It was always their expressed intention to walk in clearer light as it comes" (Gray Jan. 7, 1950). We are to marvel, not mimic, to respect, not reverence a giant like Warner.

Even so, having admitted freely that "he had his weaknesses and his limitations," John Smith points to Warner's "strengths which tower high above his failures and shortcomings." "One cannot," Smith concludes, "become well acquainted with this man's life without feeling that he [or she] has come in contact with a great soul" (July 25, 1965, 12).

What then are the essential principles that can give a movement the "flexibility and spirit of progress by which it adjusts itself as God gives light"? Byers lists four that catch up the vision and teachings of Warner. Regarding the Church of God movement:

1. It teaches the Scriptural process of salvation, by which people may obtain a real deliverance from sin and have the Holy Spirit as a witness to their salvation;

2. The truth only, and obedience thereto, is its motto; and it recognizes the rule of the Holy Spirit in the organization and government of the church;

3. It does not assume to possess all the truth, but stands committed thereto, holding an open door to the entrance of any further light and truth;

4. The spirit of the movement is to acknowledge good wherever found and to regard no door into the church other than salvation and no test of fellowship other than true Christianity possessed within the heart. Thus its basis is as narrow as the New Testament on the one hand, and as broad as the New Testament on the other (24).[4]

In addition to cautions and principles, one should note method, especially the method of music. Like John and Charles Wesley in the eighteenth century, Daniel Warner in the nineteenth century did much to help carry the reformation work on the wings of inspiring and instructing song. Thus, "any attempt to tell the story of Warner and the movement so intimately related to his ministry must give major attention to how the message was hymned" (Phillips 1974, July 14, 7).[5] Vision is carried by more than planning and church programs. There must be thoughtful worship celebration that captures the story and embraces the whole person.

Like Warner, one must add poetry to the prose, power to the programs. The story of God's ongoing work in the world is to be rehearsed and celebrated in joyous, community-building song.

Beyond method always lies the more fundamental issue of vision and intent. The goal of spiritual "experience," while central, should never be reduced to "religious satisfaction, nor personal fulfillment, nor some kind of individual experiential ecstasy." Although the spiritual journey may well lead to all of these, the objective is "that we contribute vigor and hope and service to the Body of Christ, the church, which then makes this new life available to the whole world" (Grubbs 16). The point of being holy and united as God's people is effective mission in the world.

Early in his ministry, Warner mistrusted and opposed sanctification preaching because he sensed in it hypocrisy, self-centeredness, and no positive implications for the strength, wholeness, and mission of the church. The reason for Christian unity does not lie in itself, but in the church's mission. Christians are to be one so that the world may know. The proof of Christian faith is less in how we "feel" and talk, and more in how we value, relate, and walk. Note this important assessment:

> As was true with John Wesley, Warner's emphasis was not on experience for experience sake, or for emotional ecstasy, or for some "sign" of the Spirit's coming. The classic Wesleyan stress was on dedication in depth, the purification of the motivational depths of a Christian's whole being, the flooding of a life with holy love for God and fellowman, and subsequent power for work and witness, as well as an inner sense of being at peace with God. The stress was more ethical than emotional (Phillips Sept. 22, 1974, 8).

Rather than merely a human improvement society, the body of the redeemed is God's church!

Extending the Vision

Among the many revivalists, reformers, and holiness exponents of the nineteenth century, the larger Christian community has not regarded Warner as a prominent figure. For example, Justo Gonzalez has written the widely acclaimed *A History of Christian Thought,* with volume three subtitled *From the Protestant Reformation to the Twentieth Century* (1987). Such an extensive presentation, however, does not even mention the name of Daniel Warner. This would be of no concern to Warner. The real issue is, as it was for him a century ago, our willingness as believers to be renewed by and fully obey the Spirit of God.

Pioneers like Daniel Warner, while in part shaped by and limited to their times, still have a prophetic word for us today. Consider this:

> The pioneers were so right! Even more urgently than in the 1880s, God wills today that the church be "open at the top," and that God's people be free to follow the Spirit's leading, unencumbered by institutionalism and human devisements; that faithful men and women respond with dedication and vigor to the Spirit's persistent call to renewal and mission in the light of today's urgent needs; that with candor and honesty we accept our oneness with all true Christians and consequently work out our relationships with others in the context of our common commitment; and finally, that we earnestly seek the continuing guidance of the Holy Spirit in regard to the role God would have us play in the realization of unity among all the people of God, courageously resolving to follow that guidance regardless of the consequences.... The Movement's reason for being is really no different now that it was in the beginning: to make the Church of God visible and effectual. (J. Smith 1967, 10)

Warner was not an innovator in the sense that he claimed to invent or discover truth previously unknown to the church. Rather, he was a rediscoverer, reaffirmer, re-experiencer, one who took seriously what had been basic all along. He listened to God, believed God, wanted God's word and will to be all in all. It's God's church!

Warner stands squarely in the long tradition of Anabaptism or the Believers' Church. He "scorned the lordship of the bishop and of the king in the church and fostered spiritual democracy under the doctrine of the universal priesthood of believers" (Brown, 1951, 84).

He was even a "sectarian" in the more modern, sociological sense. "Sects" can be seen positively as "radical movements, vehement in their negative reaction to church and to at least part of society." Often they are much needed by nominal and drifting church bodies. In the ongoing process of renewal, "we should recognize in the sects the fountain of our own being" (Clear, 1963, 74). Roger Williams in exile, John Wesley in England, the Geneva period of John Calvin, the experience of William Fox, the "flying ministry" of Daniel Warner, all have been needed and used by God.

In fact, there always is concern that a radical voice soon will settle into the mainstream, become comfortable, passive, and silent. For instance, "Pentecostalism," a major reforming force among Christians in the twentieth century, now has moved toward establishment status. It has been said that "every Pentecostal denomination ultimately replaces founding prophets with ruling priests; the time comes when the fear of 'wild fire' comes to outweigh a desire not to 'quench the Spirit' " (Crews, xii).[6]

Put in the specific context of the Church of God movement, certainly a Spirit-oriented reforming force, the concern is that the prophetic fire of Daniel Warner now may be supplanted by the paralyzed fumes of endless church bureaucracy. Merle Strege puts this in terms of "sages" being replaced by "managers" (1991, 119–135). Val Clear (1977, chaps. 6–7) describes it in sociological terms as "the new group becomes institutionalized" and "sophistication develops." Learning is vital, but human arrogance in place of divine wisdom is lethal.

We who believe are privileged to be members of the church only by God's grace. Our life is in Christ. Our power is only by the Spirit. Our hope lies in knowing and doing the will of God. We are Christ's one family, intended to be separated unto God—made holy—and united together in love, so that the world may know the good news of God in Christ. This was Daniel Warner's vision and burden. It became his story.

Is this your story? Will you live the life of Christ without compromise, no matter what you must face? Will you dare to reach your hands in fellowship to all who belong to Christ, building bridges and not walls? Is your commitment complete? You need an assurance like Warner's that the yoke of Christ is easy and that his burden in light in spite of all obstacles.

A Moment Then, A Moment Now

It was one of those rare moments of insight and inspiration. In its own quiet, but crucial way it brought a turning point in the history of the church in modern times. The day was December 13, 1877. A spiritually hungry Christian man took a walk in the woods to commune with God. His name was Daniel Warner. Who he was, however, now is less important than what happened next.

Warner thought much on that mild and fair day about the meaning of a person making a covenant with God. God already had acted, provided, invited. Now it was the turn of repentant women and men like himself to enter into a wonderfully available, divine-human agreement that would change and direct all of life. As he lingered reflectively in that isolated place, Warner recalled those words of divine promise found in Jeremiah 31:33—"They shall be my people." His response? Somehow it just burst with joy and new resolve out of the depths of his tender soul. "Amen, Lord, I am forever thine!"

That indeed was a sacred moment. Soon it led to a fresh wave of evangelistic sharing and the sacrificial publishing of a little paper edited by Warner and called the *Gospel Trumpet*. This Christian publication carried a note of urgency and the weight of a major mission. The mission grew directly out of the editor's radical covenant with a holy God who had called him and now was enabling this servant to live a humble, yet bold life of holiness.

Radical in this case did not mean extremism, strange new ideas that were unbiblical and outside the mainstream of classical Christian faith. Rather, it signaled a burst of new spiritual insight, energy, and commitment to what always had been, or at least always should have been, foundational to a biblically informed and Spirit–inspired faith. This "radicalism" was calling for a going back to Christian basics, back to the Bible, back to the very roots of the faith itself. The cry was for authenticity. The desire was to see again in the lives of Christians and in the life of the church itself a profound differ-

Original Gospel Trumpet building,
later renamed Warner Press

Warner Press, Anderson, Indiana, today

(above) The Church of God college in Florida, located in Lake Wales.

(left) Warner Auditorium, on the International Convention grounds, Anderson, IN. Its unique architecture is the center-piece for the annual ingathering of Church of God people.

(above) The dorm and meeting rooms on the Warner Camp grounds, located on the shores of Lake Lester in Grand Junction, MI.

(above) McGuire Auditorium on the campus of Warner Pacific College, Portland, OR, established in 1937 as Pacific Bible College.

ence from the world. The longing was for the fruit of God's redeeming presence—salvation, healing, and a unity among believers that is not possible except by the grace of God.

The prophetic call was to fresh commitment. The need was for an uncompromising covenant with God, one that brings a piercing spotlight on the frailties of the church and enables the church to function as the body of Christ.

Circumstances, of course, are somewhat different today. Yes, these holiness pioneers of a past generation had their limitations and excesses, things we hardly want to resurrect and duplicate in our current culture. But they also had a vision, a burden, a sacred covenant with God, the very things for which the church today cries out! Maybe it is time to take another quiet walk in the woods, joining Warner in order to commune there with God and enter into a covenant of holiness that can lead to unity and mission.

One thing that God still requires is our commitment as believers to a holy covenant with the divine. We are to be holy even as God is holy. There is to be a resulting passion on our part to get out the word, being both cautious and courageous in the face of much that parades falsely under the name "church." God's people are not to be more of the problem, seductive with a false spirituality, speaking in archaic language, hidden in hallowed halls, and busy with religious rituals while many people lie along Jericho roads waiting for compassionate attention. God expects a radically committed church that is not playing churchly games, gathering millions of dollars for questionable purposes, and using its strength dividing and competing with itself.

The church *of God* is the one that is set apart by God and for God, holy, carrying the message of new life to a lost world. To bear a credible witness, the church must make obvious and visible the wonderful fruits of "full salvation," including a concrete realization of oneness among all the members—so that the world may know.

That December day in 1877 surely was a rare time. It belonged in the tradition of what had happened earlier to

John Wesley in London, England. Wesley and Warner each became convinced that God had revealed the essence of the divine character as holiness (Lev. 11:45) and that God desires a separated people, holy as God is holy (1 Pet. 1:15–16). Salvation is not understood clearly or lived rightly unless it produces an actual change in people's lives, and thus a change in the life of the church and of the world. The divine invitation and challenge is for us to be holy, to enter into sacred covenant, to be set apart for God, to begin reflecting God's character as individuals and as the whole church.

Accordingly, John Smith helpfully summarizes the central burden of the Church of God movement by referring to its history as "the quest for holiness and unity" (1980). Today one might well summarize this way the need of the whole church: (1) to understand the biblical meanings of Christian holiness; (2) to experience that holiness in covenant with a holy God; and (3) to find in the wonder of this experience the vision, unity, and power necessary for believers truly to be God's children, united and on mission in this world.

The Quest Goes On

Daniel Warner was not an arriver. He was a journeyer. His home was never the ruts of a compromised status quo. He was only at home when in the process of reaching for all of God's truth, being open to all of God's grace, seeking to be all that God intends. In his first book, Warner lists five "facts" that appeared to him evident from biblical teaching. They summarize much of his later teaching.

1. The division of the Church into sects is one of Satan's most effectual, if not the very greatest means of destroying human souls;

2. Its enormous sin must be answered for by individual adherents to, and supporters of sects;

3. The only remedy for this dreadful plague is thorough sanctification, and this is only wrought by a personal,

individual contact with the blood of Christ through faith;

4. The union required by the Word of God is both a spiritual and visible union;

5. The divisions of the Church are caused by elements that are foreign to it, by deposits of the enemy, which exist in the hearts and practices of individual members, involving their responsibility and requiring their personal purgation (1880, 430–32).

Having reviewed this pattern of thought, this burden that launched a movement now worldwide in scope, six propositions now have been set forth. They seek to link Warner's reforming legacy to the challenges facing today's church. They offer insight and hope to the church today.

1. Believers in holiness must not be too ready to accept easy answers in rationalizing division in the church. Even "liberal" Christians pray God's forgiveness for participating in the sin of division;

2. A passionate concern for personal sanctification should not subvert an equally great concern for the doctrine of the church. It is well to keep in mind that the Apostle Paul uses the word sanctify in regard to both persons and the church;

3. In the light of Christ's prayer for the church (John 17), the concepts of "spiritual unity" and "invisible oneness" are inadequate and inconsistent with the apparent implications of "perfect love."

4. Associationalism and conciliarism are abortive approaches to Christian unity in that they only mitigate the evils of division and do not remove it;

5. Nondenominationalism is an inadequate concept for the full realization of Christian unity in that it expresses primarily a negative rather than a positive character to the church;

6. This time in Christian history seems to be an especially propitious one for all proponents of holiness to dedicate themselves to giving major attention to the relational implications of this doctrine to the end that, under the leadership of the Holy Spirit, we may be able to lead the way toward unification of the whole church so that, indeed, the world may believe (J. Smith, 1975, 35–36).

Daniel Warner sought to implement in a holiness environment the so-called "Protestant principle." This principle "systematically forbids anything human the place of ultimacy in the church. No creed, no organizational structure, no person or

Sidney and Birdie Warner

group of persons, no custom or habit, no idea, nothing human is to be allowed supremacy" (Bassett 8). It's God's church!

What is said of Thomas Muntzer seems to apply well to Warner and other pioneer leaders of the Church of God movement. Muntzer was a "revolutionary between the Middle Ages and modernity," a man knowing that "the old was in decay and the new was in gestation."[7] Even so, "his theology was really only a theology of revolutionary transformation and not a theology of the construction of a postrevolutionary state of affairs." We must move beyond the inspiration of restorationist rhetoric to the perspiration of finding practical ways to function more as a reformation movement (actively re-forming what ought to be). If a true church "movement" is by definition dynamic, naturally always in motion, experimenting its way toward the fulfillment of God's future, then it should be able to adapt to change more easily than highly structured and creedal bodies. To this flexible freedom and contemporary relevance the lingering legacy of Warner gladly points.

Such pointing, however, often has led to little progress. The twentieth century has seen dramatic new attention given by the Christian community around the world to the problems of Christian disunity. But the Church of God movement has chosen not to be involved for the most part. Why? There has been at least a trace of arrogance. There has been some fear of becoming contaminated by excessive public association with Christians who hold beliefs not thought biblical by the movement. There has been much insistence that the movement not support the apparent preoccupation of Christians with solving the disunity problem the wrong way. Theological compromises and denominational mergers are not the biblical answer. Unity must be rooted in holiness. See Appendix H for one recent attempt by the Church of God movement in North America to state unity guidelines.

The center is Christian mission. Holiness enables authentic unity, which in turn increases a credible witness to the world. The authority and power all belong to God. In fact, it's God's church!

Questions for Group Discussion

1. Is the early teaching of the Church of God movement about holiness and unity overly idealistic and thus not practical? Can it be understood and actually implemented today?

2. It is said that we now are in the "constructive" stage of the Lord's work of church reform. What is one specific potential action that would be genuinely constructive today? Are you prepared to take such action?

3. Regarding authority in church belief and practice, what is the meaning of being "as narrow as the New Testament on the one hand, and as broad as the New Testament on the other"? Can the church be "open at the top" and still have needed conviction and identity?

4. From 1987 to 1991 the Church of God movement in North America sponsored a "Task Force on Governance and Polity" (see Barry Callen 1992, *Thinking*, 110–111). Its final report to the General Assembly highlighted the tension between authority and accountability in church life. How can the people of God organize the work of ministry and the life of the church itself without violating the vision of Warner (or, more importantly, the very nature of the church as intented by Christ)?

5. In June 1994, Warner Press unveiled a significantly revised format for *Vital Christianity* (successor to the *Gospel Trumpet* of Warner). In part the changes hoped to renew this magazine's historic role of informing, inspiring, and holding together the Church of God movement. What really holds God's people together in changing times? Is there still a compelling gospel to proclaim, a special cause to "trumpet"?

6. Has the Church of God movement settled down into a standard denominational pattern of its own? In the section of this chapter called "The Quest Goes On," is there something that can put "move" back into the movement?

Notes

1. Merle Strege, *Vital Christianity* (January, 1990), 17. Recall, however, that Sarah's public letter denouncing her husband's teaching focuses primarily on her criticism of the narrow attitudes she claimed had overwhelmed the come-outism thrust of Warner's teaching. She herself testified to being sanctified. Note verse 29 of Warner's poem "The Alien" (1890) about Sarah and their marriage:

> My soul had longed for more of God,
> More glory in the cross;
> But, never dreamed that it must come
> Through such a bitter loss.

2. In 1903, for instance, W. G. Schell, the prominent early minister of the Church of God movement who was chosen to preach at Daniel Warner's funeral in 1895, ran into trouble with the movement. The congregation in Moundsville, West Virginia (where the Gospel Trumpet Company then was located), declared him "unworthy of their fellowship, and unfit for this ministry" ("Departed from the Faith," *Gospel Trumpet,* June 18, 1903). Schell was said to no longer believe that the Church of God movement was of God. Historian Merle Strege emphasizes that Schell, not believing that the movement's origins and message were demonic, "had come to believe, rather, that social and cultural, not to say biographical factors had shaped the movement's message" (*Vital Christianity,* August, 1994, 35).

3. A continuation of this line of evaluation is the masters thesis of Barry Callen titled "Church of God Reformation Movement (Anderson, Ind.): A Study in Ecumenical Idealism" (Asbury Theological Seminary, 1969).

4. Several sources are helpful in their attempts to restate or assess Warner's view of Christian holiness and unity. In the bibliography below, note especially Charles Brown (1939), Andrew Byers (1921), Barry Callen (1969), Aubrey Forrest

(1948), Kenneth Jones (1985), James Massey (1979), John Smith (1954), John Smith (1975), John Smith (1980), Gilbert Stafford (1973), John Stanley (1990), and Merle Strege (1991).

5. The most extensive treatments include Robert Adams (1980), Axchie Bolitho (1942), and Kathleen Buehler (1993).

6. This concern is voiced in the Crews volume with immediate reference to the Church of God (Cleveland, Tenn). Ronald Osborn, representative of the Disciples restorationist tradition, proposes eight renewal emphases crucial if the church is to react appropriately in a troubled time when it is being disestablished by the secular culture. He warns that "if we have lately fallen unwittingly into the inappropriate mindset of an ecclesiastical establishment, this essay is a call to repent and bring forth the fruits of reformation before it is too late ("The Irony of the Twentieth-Century Christian Church [Disciples of Christ]: Making It to the Mainline Just at the Time of its Disestablishment," *Mid-Stream,* July 1989, p. 312).

7. Hans-Jurgen Goertz, "Thomas Muntzer: Revolutionary Between the Middle Ages and Modernity," in *Mennonite Quarterly* Review (January 1990).

Appendix A

Innocence:

Poetic Reflection on Childhood and Spiritual Quest

by Daniel S. Warner

These autobiographical verses were composed by Daniel Warner and recited by him on the occasion of the last day of school, May 31, 1895, at the Children's Home in Grand Junction, Michigan. This was just months before his death. They are self-descriptions of Warner's own experience from childhood innocence into sin, and from sin to the glory of salvation in Christ— "innocence" regained by grace. The intent is to witness to the power of the enemy "to deceive poor souls and lead them astray," and also to show "the wonderful power there is in the blood of Christ to redeem from all sin" (Warner, 1896, Preface). The subtitles are added for reader convenience. The places where verses of this lengthy poem are omitted are indicated as "*****."

Innocence of Infancy

To thee, celestial Innocence,
   I sing my happy song.
O precious treasure in my breast,
   Thy praise I shall prolong.

Thy smile of beauty, so divine,
   Is on each infant face.
In youthful eyes thy brilliant sign,
   The angels love to trace.

To-day my childhood Innocence
  Comes back in sweet review,
As I in memory retrace
  My years of fifty-two.

Conceived in sin; to sorrow born;
  Unwelcome here on earth;
The shadows of a life forlorn,
  Hung gloomy o'er my birth.

A mother's heart, oppressed with grief,
  A father's wicked spleen,
Who cursed my faint and gasping breath,
  Combine to paint the scene.

But life held on its tender thread,
  Days, unexpected grew
To weeks: and still he lived.
  Why, Heaven only knew.

He lived, though life was bitter gain,
  His youth a flood of tears.
His body doomed to cruel pain,
  His mind, to nervous fears.

*****

If angels blessed his thorny path,
  It may be said in truth.
But two e'er showed their smiling face,
  In all his suffering youth.

One was his mother, ever kind—
   A blessed providence.
The other pure and lovely friend,
   Was angel Innocence.

He never knew that "Father" was
   A sweet endearing name.
Its very mention was a dread,
   His life's most deadly bane.

The demon of intemp'rance there,
   Infused the wrath of hell.
And most upon this sickly head
   The storm of fury fell.

Like chickens when the mother bird
   Gives signal of a foe,
Her little peeps are quickly hushed,
   All chicks are lying low.

So, when returning from the town,
   The dreaded steps we heard,
All ran and quickly settled down,
   And not a lip was stirred.

O horrors of the liquor fiend!
   We've seen thy hell on earth.
Thy serpent coils around us twined,
   The moment of our birth.

O Rum, thy red infernal flame—
  I witness to the truth—
Filled all my mother's cup with pain,
  And swallowed up my youth.

But yet, in all the wretchedness
  Of those primeval years,
The blessing of meek Innocence,
  Dropped sweetness in my tears.

By Sin Beguiled

Then suddenly a crisis came
  In this poor trembling breast.
While treading life's poor narrow lane,
  A solemn line I passed.

Within my bosom there awoke
  A monitor of light:
Anon I heard it loudly speak,
  "Fear God and do the right."

Ere long the helpless spirit felt
  An arrow pierce within.
And then, alas! the sting of guilt
  Came with the dart of sin.

And sin, the woeful monster, brought
  Death as its recompense.
O sin! O death! ye have despoiled
  My soul of Innocence.

*****

Like roses smitten by the frost;
  So childhood, stung by sin.
Lo! every outward charm is lost,
  And dead, the soul within.

My fettered spirit, borne along
  By sin's infernal sway;
The melancholy of my soul
  Grew darker day by day.

*****

As evil habits daily grew,
  They, by satanic skill,
Were catenated into chains,
  That bound my soul for hell.

O wretched state! O horrid doom!
  O fate, reverse thy train,
Return, O time! and bear me back,
  To childhood's dream again.

But why send out my hopeless cry,
  Upon the empty wind?
Alas! pure Innocence is gone, and I
  No tranquil rest may find.

I stood beside the sea of life—
  So dark and turbulent—
Where hopes of men by sin are wrecked,
  And heard their sad lament.

I saw the youth, whose restless feet
  By sin had been beguiled;
And, tired of the empty fraud,
  He wished himself a child.

I saw the aged sinner writhe
  Beneath the weight of years,
Alarmed by death's approaching scythe,
  And judgment's awful fears.

Redeeming Love of Jesus

O could I hear them sing once more!
  Even that angel, sweet,
That in my childhood hovered o'er
  The pathway of my feet.

[Singing in the distance]

"There's mercy, poor sinner, for thee,
  And Jesus will banish thy gloom;
Salvation is offered so free,
  All heaven invites thee to come."

[Chorus]

"O come, will you come to the Lord?
  Will you come and be saved in Jesus' blood?
Will you come? will you come and be free?
  O the Savior so kindly calleth thee."

"O wonderful, wonderful love,
  That Jesus has suffered and died;
And now he is pleading above,
  O come to the once Crucified."

"Lo! Jesus thy Savior and Friend,
  Now stands at the door of thy heart;
So gentle, so loving and kind,
  Admit him, lest grieved he depart."

"O welcome the Savior to form
  His kingdom of glory within;
He'll enter thy bosom to reign,
  And banish all sorrow and sin."

O angel of mercy and love,
  Thy beauty on me shine;
Bring Innocence down from above,
  Come, take this heart of mine.
*****

I sink by love o'ercome.
*****

Return of Innocence

And now I turned my eyes within,
  And, lo, there sat on throne,
The same sweet angel, Innocence,
  I had in childhood known.

She came so softly in the train,
  Came and resumed her place;
Amid the raptures of the scene,
  I scarce perceived her grace.

O Innocence! my heart o'erflows!
  Hast thou returned at last?
O pardon me for all the foes
  That drove thee from my breast!
                    *****
I am once more a child. 'Tis true;
  This is no fancy dream.
'Neath Heaven's smile I launch anew
  On life's pure crystal stream.

To-day I look without remorse,
  Up in my Father's face;
And feel as free as first I smiled,
  In mother's fond embrace.

As free from consciousness of sin
  As angels in their sphere,
Who never felt the cursed sting,
  Nor shed one bitter tear.

And, looking back on life's career,
  All, all is 'neath the blood,
And then I hear sweet Innocence
  Sing out her praise to God.

The future, too, has no appal.
  The awful judgment day,
Bright Innocence awaits with joy,
  And sings the time away.

And when I cast my eyes to heaven,
  No shame can paint a blush.
The angels shout, "A soul forgiven,"
  But thoughts of sin all hush.

A new-born soul. I stand and gaze
  With rapture and delight,
Amid a new creation, filled
  With beams of sacred light.

For He that sits upon the throne
  Declares, I make all new—
New heavens and earth I find,
  In Christ it all is true.

Within my heart where dragons lay,
  Now angel graces sing.
And Innocence has come to stay,
  Since Jesus in my king.

Appendix B

Editorial Statement, Herald of Gospel Freedom, 1879

by Daniel S. Warner and I. W. Lowman

The early theological perspectives of Daniel Warner can be seen in the 1879 prospectus prepared for the *Herald of Gospel Freedom* by I. W. Lowman, editor and publisher, and D. S. Warner, associate editor. In part the 1879 statement read:

As heretofore, it shall be the aim of the *Herald* to "contend earnestly for the faith once delivered to the saints," not a part, but the whole faith of the gospel, ignoring the traditions of men, reproving the works of darkness and enforcing all the will of God.

It believes in raising men to the Bible standard of holy living by leading them into the Bible measure of grace.

It advocates a salvation that lifts men above the regions of mere duty and places them in such sweet and perfect harmony with God that they delight to do his will; a salvation that constrains to every good work by the infinite power of perfect love, and not by the lash of the law.

Viewed from a human standpoint the *Herald* may appear to possess two separate features; namely, that of an organ of the Church of God and an advocate of holiness. But viewed from a pure Bible standpoint these distinct features naturally blend into one effort to restore and propagate the pure religion of the Bible.

Church signifies "called out." The divinely given title, Church of God, therefore denotes the called out of God or separated unto God. Holiness means the same thing; that is, to be separated from all sin and wholly given up to God.

The editors of the *Herald* firmly believe that apostolic truths and Bible holiness cannot be separated.

The work of holiness has been too long encumbered by human creeds and disintegrated parties among its friends.

Though holiness as a distinct experience is the most precious and important truth of the gospel, its wonderful triumphs have been much limited and rendered comparatively unstable for the want of being identified with all other Bible truths and divested of human systems.

Upon the other hand, the Church, ever accepting the only infallible and divinely authorized standard of discipline and wearing the only church title that was "given by the mouth of the Lord," is utterly disqualified to perform her appointed mission in bringing the world to God unless she be girded with the invincible power of perfect holiness and the full and distinct baptism of the Holy Ghost.

Truth is mighty; but holiness, being the fullness of God in man, is almighty. The union of these divine forces, we believe, will make a complete conquest of this world for God.

To restore the divine plan in harmonious action and the spread of these elements of salvation is the primary object of the *Herald*. A part of the paper will therefore be devoted especially to that doctrine and experience of entire sanctification, to be conducted by the Associate Editor, the Editor-in-Chief being also fully in line with holiness definitely through the blood.

With an unshaken trust in God, and confiding in the integrity of our cause and the support of all lovers of truth and Christian purity, we begin Vol. II of the *Herald* in the name of the Lord Jesus.

Appendix C

"The Kind of Power Needed to Carry the Holiness Work"
Presentation to the Western Union Holiness Convention, Jacksonville, Illinois, December, 1880

by Daniel S. Warner

The following are key paragraphs from this presentation by Daniel Warner. The full text is available in the published proceedings of the convention.

It seems to me that God proposes to utilize all the powers of his universe to spread holiness. He will hasten it in His time. We want the old-fashioned power in the work. The Savior said, "Tarry ye until ye be endued with power from on high." It is the power of God Himself that is needed for this work. It is through the Holy Ghost that God brings this power to bear upon us, and upon our work.

The prophet Micah said, "I am full of power by the Spirit of the Lord, and of judgment and of might, to declare unto Jacob his transgressions, and to Israel his sin." We are told it is "not by might, nor by power; but by my Spirit, saith the Lord." The power that originally moved upon the face of the elements to create all things, that Power is recreating all things today. We recognize the same power that Micah had to declare to Israel his sins; to declare the whole counsel of God.

It is more important that we have power to deal faithfully with men, than that we have a flow of emotion. The power of the Holy Ghost is so indispensable to this holiness work, that there is no efficiency without it. We should wake up to the fact that we have no right to go until we have this power. We ought not to sanction one's going, when the Spirit says, stay at home until endued with the power. It is this Holy Ghost unction that intensifies all our powers, and electrifies our entire being, so that when thus anointed, we then will preach the gospel, with the Holy Spirit sent down from heaven.

It seems to me that God is looking around to find some one He can trust. He generally finds them among the holy ones. If God can't get a large vessel, He will take a small one. God can put more pure salvation in a pint cup that is clean than a bushel measure that is not. Christ must be revealed in us as our Sanctifier.

We need the gospel measure spoken of in 2 Thessalonians: "Wherefore we pray always for you, that our God would count you worthy of this calling, and fulfill all the pleasure of this goodness, and the work of faith with power." It is the pleasure of his goodness that the sinner be converted; and that the believer be sanctified. The Lord helps us to give the Spirit the right of way! "That the name of our Lord Jesus Christ be glorified in you, and we in him."

The devil is set against this work. He has a mighty array of talent and power; and we need God's power to the fullest degree promised, to meet this adversary.

As I said at the beginning, it is the power of God—the power of the Holy Ghost we need! The Holy Ghost is God; and it is God that worketh all in all. Faith is the upreaching act of the soul by which we grasp the power of God. He does not require a great deal from you; only that you will be where you can appreciate His power for the good of His cause, and the glory of His name.

Appendix D

"My Lovely Little Levilla Modest"

From the personal journal of Daniel Warner, on the death of his beloved daughter, Levilla Modest, June 1878

Then we looked for the last time upon our beloved child whose sweet and innocent little form, dressed in its little white dress and skirts, with a beautiful little bouquet of flowers protruding from her little hands folded upon her breast. As my dear wife was deeply afflicted with her departure, her sweet little face seemed to speak forth from its little white coffin and say, "Weep not, dear Mother, for though your loss seems to be great, my gain is infinitely greater. I have gone to the better land where sickness, sorrow, pain, and death never come."

We laid the dear and only child in the Mission Cemetery at Upper Sandusky near the road at the west side between two evergreens. There, with sad, yet resigned hearts, we left her to sleep beneath the angels' care until called forth at the last day.

Levilla Modest was born March 18, 1875, near Seward, Nebraska. She passed from suffering to the society of angels June 24, 1878.... She was very knowing about all kinds of work and ever eager to assist. For some months in the past she would stand upon a chair beside her mother and wipe knives, forks, spoons, saucers, etc., with the utmost care and perfection. She would do the most of her dressing and undressing and never failed to hang up or put away every garment and everything she handled. She seemed to have very fine taste and perfect order.....

Since 18 months old she would sing parts of familiar tunes and hymns. I believe her first was "Happy Day." For some time past she would tread the organ with one foot, place her little fingers upon the keys and sing loudly "Hallelujah 'Tis Done," "I Am Washed in the Blood of the Lamb," etc. She had a remarkable tendency to imitate all that was pure and religious. She often had her little prayer meetings by herself and would teach older children when with her to engage with her in her childish prayers and songs.

After attending an ordinance meeting where she paid marked attention to the saints washing feet, the next day she called for a wash bowl of water and washed her feet, then took off her mother's shoes and stockings and washed and wiped her feet and gave her a kiss. Every evening she knelt at her mother's knee and said her little prayer.... Her love seemed to possess the purity and strength of one fully renewed in the image of God, and yet the innocence and simplicity of a child. As she placed those precious little arms around our neck and gave the warm kiss, we could not help but feel that this was real and not mere child's play, and those embraces were free for all who sought them.

> But who can ever, ever tell
> The sweetness of that dear one,
> Too celestial on earth to dwell,
> More at home with angel throng.
>
> All free from sin for Heaven meet,
> Our dear Levilla Modest,
> Has found a safe and sure retreat
> Within the Savior's bosom.
>
> We miss the dear through all the day,
> And when falls the evening shade,
> Sacred every playful mark
> Thy innocent hands have made.

Thy little bed and vacant chair,
Thy toys, picture books and gown,
With all the clothes thou here did wear
Seem to wish for thy return.

Gone, thy sweet spirit, pure and white
From earthly sin and sorrow,
To realms of never-ending light,
Where days shall have no morrow.

We've laid thee where soft shadows creep,
On each side an evergreen,
There calmly rest in dreamless sleep,
Evermore by angels seen.

Appendix E

"To My Dear Sidney"

Poem of grief and hope by Daniel Warner, addressed to
Sidney, his young son, following the departure of Sarah
Warner, their wife and mother. (As found on pages 182–186
of Daniel Warner, Poems of Grace and Truth.)

> The heart that feels a father's love,
>   And swells with love's return,
> Will kindly bear this overflow,
>   Toward my only son.
>
> Yes, Sidney's love so blent with mine,
>   A poem shall employ;
> A token left to coming time,
>   That father loved his boy.
>
> One gentle vine, thy tendrils sweet,
>   Around my soul entwine.
> A comfort left in sorrows deep,
>   One heart to beat with mine.
>
> Thy life has dawned in peril's day,
>   Mid wars that Heaven shake;
> Thy summers five, eventful, they
>   Like surges o'er thee break.

Thy little soul has felt the shock,
  Of burning babel's fall;
When hell recoiled in fury black,
  And stood in dread appall.

But wreaking out his vengeance now,
  Like ocean's terror dark;
Hell's monster came athwart the Bow
  Of our domestic bark.

Thy guardian angel wept to see
  This brunt of fury sweep
The girdings of maternity
  From underneath thy feet.

But pity still her garlands weave
  Around thy gentle brow;
And angels on thee softly breathe
  Their benedictions now.

They soothe and bless thy manly heart,
  And wipe away thy tears.
So tempered to thy bitter lot,
  The bitter sweet appears.

An exile now is each to each;
  As banished far at sea.
A martyr on his island beach,
  I daily think of thee.

And stronger love has seldom spanned
  The mocking billows, wild,
Than are the chords that ever bind
  To my beloved child.

Though sundered not by angry main,
  Compelled from thine embrace;
We flee abroad in Jesus' name,
  To publish Heaven's grace.

Thy little heart cannot divine,
  Why pappa stays away.
But coming years will tell—if thine—
  The great necessity.

When sickness crushed thy little form,
  I knew my boy was ill;
I heard thee in my visions call,
  But duty kept me still.

A trial deep, to feel thy pain,
  And yet debarred from thee,
To show that sinners lost, were it
  A greater misery.

O may this lesson speak to thee,
  When father's work is done;
And highest may thy glory be,
  A soul for God is won.

And now my son, attentive hear,
  My benediction prayer,
And ever tune thy heart and ear,
  To Heaven's music, rare.

For ere the light of day had shone,
  In thy unfolding eyes;
We gave thee up to God alone,
  A living sacrifice.

And oft repeated when a babe,
  To God our child was giv'n;
And Jesus heard the vow we made,
  And wrote it down in Heav'n.

So like a little Samuel, you
   Must answer, "Here am I."
Give all your heart to Jesus too,
   For Him to live and die.

Like Samuel, serve the living God,
   His temple be thy home,
In love obey His holy Word:
   Thy gentle heart His throne.

The Lord is good, my darling boy,
   He touched thy body well,
And He will bless thee ever more,
   If in His love you dwell.

A new edition may you be,
   Of father's love and zeal,
But enlarged so wondrously,
   That earth thy tread may feel.

Appendix F

Proposed Consolidation of the Northern Indiana Eldership of the Churches of God and the Evangelical United Mennonite Church

Daniel Warner participated actively in seeking to bring a formal union ("merger") between these two church bodies. His journal entry of December 5, 1879, reports: "The subject of consolidation was warmly advocated from both sides, while our hearts glowed with the unifying 'glory' of Jesus Christ. The following preamble and resolutions were adopted at this joint meeting."

Whereas the God of all grace has most emphatically taught us in his word that his church is one, as the Father and Son are one, and that a manifestation of this unity is to be the world saving salt of the church;

Therefore, we, as the professed sons of God, and members of the United Mennonite church and the Church of God, assembled in the name of Jesus Christ in a joint meeting, do confess it our duty to put away from us every accursed thing that might in the least distract, divide and alienate us in heart or cause divergency in practice; and for the sake of securing an answer to the prayer of the adorable Saviour, we do solemnly agree to abandon anything not warranted by the word of God and accept any and every thing it teaches. Therefore,

Resolved, That we joyfully consent to the will of our Lord and Savior, Jesus Christ, and agree to unite in one body as soon as in the providence of God the consolidation can be consummated; and

Resolved, That we recognize the Word of God as the only true basis of Christian union; furthermore,

Resolved, That we believe that the "truth as it is in Christ Jesus" is within our reach, hence can be ascertained on all points of difference, and that we are therefore morally bound to learn and abide its decision.

Appendix G

We Believe

Portion of a Statement of Conviction by the Faculty and Staff of Anderson University School of Theology, on the occasion of the centennial celebration of the Church of God Movement, 1980

We believe in a cluster of biblical teachings which form a vision of the church. Specifically:

God's church is the community of redeemed persons.

It is not to be understood primarily as any or all of the humanly designed and historically conditioned organizations of Christians. It is a divinely ordered fellowship of all persons in harmonious relationship with God. A local congregation, then, is best understood as a local manifestation of the church universal (Eph. 2:14-21; 1 Cor. 1:2).

God's church is a community of divine-human partnership with Christ as Head.

The church is all of God's redeemed children. It is the people of God made members one of another under the headship of Christ (Eph. 2:19-22). It is that unique body chosen for purposeful partnership in accomplishing the will of God on earth. Persons who are admitted to membership in the church by the grace of God (Acts 2:47) and equipped for service by the gifting of God (I Cor. 12:4-7) are the Spirit-led persons who guide the life and work of the church, just as that Christian council at Jerusalem made strategic decisions in light of what "seemed good to the Holy Spirit and to us" (Acts 15:28).

God's church is a holy community.

Its holiness does not center in its possession of sacraments as means of saving grace or in its being historically in line with a hierarchically conceived "apostolic succession." It is the "Body of Christ." Through the atoning work of Christ and the sanctifying work of the Holy Spirit, the church, through the individual lives of its members, is privileged to participate in and demonstrate that holiness. (1 Cor. 1:2, 3:17; Eph. 5:25–27)

God's church is intended to be a unified community

The dividedness among Christian people today is not just unfortunate; it is inappropriate and wholly unacceptable. Unity is clearly God's will for the church. Participation in the Lord's Supper dramatizes the intended unity of Christians as they celebrate their one Lord, one salvation, and one mission. But that unity, symbolized in worship, must find visible expression in the life and witness of the church. The goal is less a contrived peace treaty among deeply divided church organizations and more a radical reconsideration of what is an appropriate network of relationships among brothers and sisters in Christ (Luke 22:14–19; John 17:20-21; Rom. 12:4–5; Gal. 3:28; Eph. 4:4).

We have committed ourselves to the implications of this vision of God's Church. A unified life and witness among brothers and sisters in Christ is not optional. It is a natural outcome of the experience of grace and membership in the body of Christ. It is a crucial factor in the effectiveness of the church on mission!

Appendix H

Inter-Church Cooperation

The General Assembly of the Church of God, Convened in Anderson, Indiana, Sessions of June 1985, through June 1988

The General Assembly of the Church of God recognized and affirmed the call issued in 1984 to the Church of God by the Consultation on Mission and Ministry of the Church of God. It was a call "to expand ministries through voluntary relationships with church groups outside the Church of God reformation movement" so that we can "achieve our mission more effectively and expand our ministries." The Assembly, between 1985 and 1988, initiated study of the biblical base of this call, specific implications of the call, especially for its national church agencies, and guidelines for proceeding. Full detail is available in *Thinking and Acting Together* (Callen, 1992, 27–30).

WORKS CITED

A Brief History of the Church of God in Alabama (White): 1891–1966. Alabama Unified Budgets Board.

Adams, Robert. 1980. "The Hymnody of the Church of God (1885–1980) as a Reflection of That Church's Theological and Cultural Changes." Doctoral dissertation. Fort Worth, Texas: Southwestern Baptist Theological Seminary.

Allen, C. Leonard and Richard Hughes. 1988. *Discovering Our Roots: The Ancestry of Churches of Christ*. Abilene, Texas: Abilene Christian University Press.

——. Leonard and Richard Hughes. 1988. *Illusions of Innocence*. University of Chicago Press.

Allison, Joseph. 1974–75 (Sept. 8 through Jan. 19). Biographical article series in *Vital Christianity*.

Bassett, Paul. 1983 (spring). "The Holiness Movement and the Protestant Principle." *Wesleyan Theological Journal*.

Berry, Robert L. 1931. *Golden Jubilee Book*. Anderson, Ind: Gospel Trumpet Co.

Bolitho, Axchie A. 1942. *To the Chief Singer* [Barney Warren]. Anderson, Ind: Gospel Trumpet Co.

Brown, Charles E. 1939. *The Church Beyond Division*. Anderson, Ind: Gospel Trumpet Co.

——. 1951. *When the Trumpet Sounded*. Anderson, Ind: Gospel Trumpet   Co.

Brown, Charles E. 1954. *When Souls Awaken: An Interpretation of Radical Christianity*. Anderson, Ind: Gospel Trumpet Co.

Buehler, Kathleen. 1993. *Heavenly Song*. Anderson, Ind: Warner Press.

Byers, Andrew. 1920. "Pioneers of the Present Reformation, D. S. Warner," *Gospel Trumpet*, Feb. 5.

——. 1921. *Birth of a Reformation: Life and Labors of D. S. Warner*. Anderson, Ind: Gospel Trumpet Co. Contains large sections of Warner's surviving personal journal.

Byrum, Noah. 1902. *Familiar Names and Faces.* Moundsville, WVa: Gospel Trumpet Co.

——. 1931–32. "Memories of Bygone Days," *Young People's Friend,* (Dec. 1931–Aug. 1932).

Caldwell, Maurice. 1992. "Milestones in the Life of the First Missionary of the Church of God" (B. F. Elliott), *Church of God Missions* (June).

Callen, Barry. 1969. "Church of God Reformation Movement (Anderson, Ind.): A Study in Ecumenical Idealism" (master's thesis, Asbury Theological Seminary).

——. 1979. *The First Century.* Vols. I and II. Anderson, Ind: Warner Press.

——. 1988. *Preparing for Service: A History of Higher Education in the Church of God.* Anderson, Ind: Warner Press.

——. 1992. *She Came Preaching.* Anderson, Ind: Warner Press.

——. 1992. *Thinking and Acting Together.* Anderson, Ind: Executive Council and Warner Press.

—— 1992. *Guide of Soul and Mind: The Story of Anderson University.* Anderson, Ind: Anderson University and Warner Press.

Churches of God: General Conference. 1986. *We Believe.* Findlay, Ohio: Churches of God Publications.

Clear, Valorous B. 1977. *Where the Saints Have Trod.* Chesterfield, Ind: Midwest Publications.

——. 1963. "Reflections of a Postsectarian." *The Christian Century* (Jan. 16).

Confer, Robert L. 1992. *Remembering, Reflecting, Renewing: A Look at the Historical Developments of the Church of God In and Around Grand Junction, Michigan.* Grand Junction: Warner Camp (for its centennial).

Crews, Mickey. 1990. *The Church of God [Cleveland, Tenn.]: A Social History.* Knoxville: University of Tennessee Press.

Crose, Lester. 1981. *Passport for a Reformation.* Anderson, Ind: Warner Press.

Cummins, Kenneth. 1974. *Dutchtown: A History of New Washington and Cranberry Township.* New Washington, Ohio: Centennial Committee.

Dayton, Donald. 1987, 1991. Rev. ed. *Theological Roots of*

Pentecostalism. Hendrickson Publishers.

Dieter, Melvin. 1980. *The Holiness Revival of the Nineteenth Century.* Metuchen, N. J: Scarecrow Press.

Doctrines and Discipline of the Evangelical United Mennonites. 1880. Goshen, Ind: E. U. Mennonite Publishing Society.

Ferrel, Lowell. 1988. "John Wesley and the Enthusiasts," in *Wesleyan Theological Journal.* (Spring/Fall).

Forney, C. H. 1914. *History of the Churches of God.* Harrisburg, Pa: Pub. House of the Churches of God—Winebrennerian.

Forrest, Aubrey. 1948. "A Study of the Development of the Basic Doctrines and Institutional Patterns in the Church of God (Anderson, Ind.)." Unpublished doctoral dissertation. University of Southern California Graduate School of Religion.

Hatch, Nathan. 1989. *The Democratization of American Christianity.* Yale University Press.

Hetrick, Gale. 1980. *Laughter Among the Trumpets: A History of the Church of God in Michigan.* Centennial Edition: The Church of God in Michigan.

History of Berrien and VanBuren Counties, Michigan. 1880. Philadelphia: D. W. Ensign & Co.

Gossard, J. Harvey. 1986. "John Winebrenner: Founder, Reformer, and Businessman" in *Pennsylvania Religious Leaders* (History Study No. 16), The Pennsylvania Historical Association.

Grubbs, Dwight. 1994. *Beginnings: Spiritual Formation for Leaders.* Fairway Press.

Jones, Kenneth. 1985. *Commitment to Holiness.* Anderson, Ind: Warner Press.

Kern, Richard. 1974. *John Winebrenner: Nineteenth Century Reformer.* Harrisburg, Pa: Central Publishing House.

Kern, Richard. 1984. *Findlay College: The First Hundred Years.* Nappanee, Ind: Evangel Press.

Littell, Franklin. 1961. "The Discipline of Discipleship in the Free Church Tradition." *Mennonite Quarterly Review.* (April).

Leonard, Juanita Evans, ed. 1989. *Called to Minister, Empowered to Serve: Women in Ministry.* Warner Press.

Long, L. Leon. 1976. "To What Extent Was Warner a

Winebrennarian?" *Church Advocate.* (Feb).

McCutcheon, Lillie. 1964. *The Symbols Speak.* Published privately.

Massey, James Earl. 1979. *Concerning Christian Unity.* Anderson, Ind: Warner Press.

Mead, Sidney. 1963. *The Lively Experiment: The Shaping of Christianity in America.* Harper & Row.

Mitchell, T. Chrichton. 1994. *Charles Wesley: Man With the Dancing Heart.* Kansas City: Beacon Hill Press.

Morrison, John. 1962. *As the River Flows* (an autobiography). Anderson, Ind: Anderson College Press.

———. 1974 (June 9 through August 25). Biographical article series in *Vital Christianity.*

Naylor, Charles. n.d. (1948?). *The Teachings of D. S. Warner and His Associates.* Published privately.

North, James. 1994. *Union In Truth: An Interpretive History of the Restoration Movement.* Cincinnati: Standard Publishing.

Phillips, Harold. 1974. Editorials in *Vital Christianity.* (June 9 through October 20).

———. 1979. *Miracle of Survival.* Anderson, Ind: Warner Press.

Proceedings of the Western Union Holiness Convention. 1881. Bloomington, Ill: Western Holiness Association.

Reardon, Robert. 1979. *The Early Morning Light.* Anderson, Ind: Warner Press.

Reid, Daniel, et. al., eds. 1990. *Dictionary of Christianity in America.* InterVarsity Press.

Riggle, Herbert. 1924. *Pioneer Evangelism.* Anderson, Ind: Gospel Trumpet Co.

Royster, James. 1967. "A History of the Church of God in South India." Master's thesis. Hartford Seminary Foundation.

Schell, William. 1893. *Biblical Trace of the Church.* Grand Junction, Mich: Gospel Trumpet Co.

Schwarz, R. W. 1979. *Light Bearers to the Remnant* (denominational textbook for Seventh-day Adventism). Boise, Idaho: Pacific Press Publishing Association.

Smith, Frederick. 1913. *What the Bible Teaches.* Anderson, Ind: Gospel Trumpet Co.

———. 1919. *The Last Reformation.* Anderson, Ind: Gospel Trumpet Co.

Smith, John. 1954. "The Approach of the Church of God

(Anderson, Ind) and Comparable Groups to the Problem of Christian Unity." Unpublished doctoral dissertation, University of Southern California Graduate School of Religion.

——. 1955. In chapter two, "D. S. Warner." *Heralds of a Brighter Day*. Anderson, Ind: Gospel Trumpet Co.

——. 1956. *Truth Marches On*. Anderson, Ind: Gospel Trumpet Co.

——. 1965 "D. S. Warner: Pioneer Leader," *Vital Christianity*. (July 11, 18, 25).

——. 1967. "The Church of God at Eighty-Six." *School of Theology Bulletin*, Anderson College [University] (spring).

——. 1975. "Holiness and Unity." *Wesleyan Theological Journal* (spring).

——. 1980. *The Quest for Holiness and Unity*. Anderson, Ind: Warner Press.

Smith, Uriah. 1882. *Thoughts, Critical and Practical, on the Books of Daniel and the Revelation*. Battle Creek, Mich: Review and Herald Press.

Snyder, Howard. 1980. *The Radical Wesley*. Downers Grove, Ill: InterVarsity Press.

Stafford, Gilbert. 1973. "Experiential Salvation and Christian Unity in the Thought of Seven Theologians of the Church of God (Anderson, Ind.)." Unpublished doctoral dissertation, Boston University School of Theology.

Stanley, John. 1990. "Unity Amid Diversity: Interpreting the Book of Revelation in the Church of God (Anderson)." *Wesleyan Theological Journal* (fall).

Starr, William H. 1857. *Discourses on the Nature of Faith and Kindred Subjects*. Chicago: D. B. Cook and Company.

Strege, Merle. 1991. *Tell Me the Tale: Historical Reflections on the Church of God*. Anderson, Ind: Warner Press.

——. 1991 "Demise (?) of a Peace Church," *Mennonite Quarterly Review*. (April).

——. 1993. *Tell Me Another Tale: Further Reflections on the Church of God*. Anderson, Ind: Warner Press.

Stroup, George. 1981. *The Promise of Narrative Theology*. Atlanta: John Knox Press.

Toulouse, Mark. 1992. *Joined in Discipleship: The Maturing of an American Religious Movement*. St. Louis: Chalice Press.

Warner, Daniel S. (his various publications are listed separately).

Wickersham, H. C. 1900. *A History of the Church.* Moundsville, WVa: Gospel Trumpet Co.

Zahniser, Clarence. 1957. *Earnest Christian: Life and Works of Benjamin Titus Roberts.* Published by author.